Prisoners of Hope

Prisoners of Hope

Turn you to the stronghold, ye prisoners of hope. Zechariah 9:12.

James and Marti Hefley

Christian Publications, Inc.

Christian Publications, Inc.
25 S. Tenth Street, Harrisburg, PA 17101

The mark of **Cp** *vibrant faith*

Library of Congress Catalog Card Number: 76-28840
©1976 Christian Publications, Inc. All rights reserved
Printed in the United States of America

Dedication

Dedicated to the Christians the missionaries left in Vietnam, with the hope that readers will be constrained to pray for them.

Authors' Note

This is a true story. Names, dates, places, and incidents are based on Betty Mitchell's diary and the remembrances of the missionaries who lived through this experience. Conversations that could not be recalled exactly are in keeping with the mood and facts of the events.

Betty and Archie Mitchell and children Becki, Glenn, Gerry, and Loretta at Bly, Oregon, in 1962. Shortly after returning to Vietnam Archie was captured by the Communists. Lillian and Richard Phillips and children Brian, Jean, John, and Ruth at the Saigon International Airport prior to the children's departure for school in Penang, Malaysia.

Joan and Norman Johnson and children Pat and Doug (insets) in Banmethuot, Vietnam, in 1974.

Carolyn and John Miller and children Gordon, LuAnne, Nate, and Margie.

Contents

1	"Shadow of the Almighty"	9
2	"Act Like Prisoners!"	29
3	Grit, Grime, and Grace	47
4	A Hard Week	63
5	Life in "Camp Sunshine"	77
6	Hurts and Heartaches	97
7	"Camp Wilderness"	117
8	Scourge of the Tropics	135
9	"Fat City"	153
10	Together Again	171
11	"Guests" in North Vietnam	189
12	Answered Prayers	209
Epilogue		235

1

"Shadow of the Almighty"

"*Aduon, Aduon*, there are VCs all around and many, many tanks in the jungle." The eyes of the lithe, young Raday tribesman rounded with apprehension as he looked up at the American missionary who towered over him.

After twenty-seven years in Vietnam, Betty Mitchell was not one to get excited at such rumors. But something about the intensity of the Raday raised her concern.

"Have they been bothering you?"

"No," came the solemn reply with a shake of the dark head.

"Then why is everyone looking sad?"

"We've heard they're going to attack Banmethuot."

A shiver ran up Betty's spine. The beautiful city in the middle of the central highlands had already known so much tragedy. Nearly every tribal family had lost a loved one. And the missionaries had lost many colleagues during their years of service in the heart of the Southeast Asian war zone.

The memories stabbed her mind: 1962, Dr. Ardel Vietti, Dan Gerber, and her own dear husband, Archie, captured at the leprosarium only twelve miles out in the jungle; 1968, six close missionary friends killed and their compound destroyed. Two others, Betty Olsen and Hank Blood, also taken captive, died of starvation and disease on the trail.

Now it was March 1975, and an uneasy "peace" hung over the land. The military had left in 1973. Everyone knew that it was just a matter of time before the Communists launched another major offensive in the South. The tribespeople were constantly reporting stories from the jungle that the North Vietnamese were bringing in heavy equipment and building roads. But what reason could they have to attack Banmethuot, a highland city far from the major population centers? Surely they would hit more strategic places first, giving advance warning for the missionaries to leave. But who could know the minds of the Communists?

Betty smiled reassuringly at the worried Raday. "Well, things are quiet enough today." The smile seemed to comfort him.

She looked around at the Raday young people she had brought in her Land Rover for the Sunday afternoon witnessing trip. How it thrilled her to see them taking over the activities: choosing who would preach or tell a Bible story and deciding what songs to sing. During the past few months through these excursions into surrounding tribal villages many had received Christ. And over three thousand decisions for Christ had been recorded in the Pocket Testament League's recent literature campaign. The spirit of revival was truly a refreshing from the Lord. She prayed it would not end in a blood bath.

The young people climbed into the Rover to be driven to the next stop. As they bounced along, Betty's voice blended with theirs in favorite gospel choruses.

Despite the differences in age and nationality, they enjoyed a close bond. She had come to Vietnam before they were born. Her love and loyalty had been tried and tested. They knew that after her husband had been captured she stayed on with no desire other than to serve Christ by serving them. Addressing her as *"aduon"* (grandmother) was the highest respect and affection they could show.

It had been a long time since Betty and Archie had left Oregon. In 1948 Vietnam was part of French Indo-China. They hadn't even known a storm was brewing until on board ship they read in a newsmagazine an article titled "The Sad Little War." It was hard to believe they were heading into a war zone until they neared Saigon and saw a body floating in the river. The shooting they heard that first night became an all too familiar sound.

After their first daughter, Becki, was born in the mountain resort city of Dalat, they journeyed to Hanoi for Vietnamese language study. They were assigned to Sontay, a small town about forty kilometers from Hanoi, when a request came to serve as houseparents in the Dalat School for missionaries' children. During this assignment, which continued through two four-year terms, three more children were born to them: Loretta, Glenn, and Gerry.

When finally they were replaced at Dalat School, the door to North Vietnam had closed to missionaries. They were sent to the leprosarium near Banmethuot, the center of Christian and Missionary Alliance outreach to thousands of Raday, Mnong, Koho, Jarai, and other tribespeople. A little more than a month later black-pajamaed Viet Cong stole from the dark jungle and took Archie, Ardel, and Dan. Ardel, the leprosarium's physician, and Dan, a Mennonite agriculturist, were single. Archie's capture left Betty and the four children to wait for his release.

Their sorrow welded them together with bonds of love and loyalty that transcended the natural ties of family. They had each other and the Lord. Together they would wait for the day when their family would once again be complete.

Perhaps it was this sorrow that enabled Betty to identify closely with the suffering tribespeople. She felt especially close to them as they rode back to Banmethuot together under a bright sun. The political future of Vietnam might be uncertain, but their trust in one another and in God was secure.

Betty left her passengers at the Raday church where she would join them for services later. Then she drove across the mission compound to her home, the middle of three neat, new bungalows built to replace the missionary homes destroyed in 1968.

The pastel shades of the modest houses were a pleasing contrast to the deep green of the expansive rolling lawn between them and Highway 14. No scars were visible of the destruction wrought in the '68 battle waged between the South Vietnamese army from behind the compound and the Communists advancing along the highway. The one silent reminder was the memorial that had been built by the tribal Christians to honor those who had given their lives there.

From the carport of her home Betty could see the columned marker that said simply:

> *In memory of those valiant missionaries who here laid down their lives during Tet 1968*
> *NATHAN ROBERT ZIEMER*
> *CARL EDWARD THOMPSON*
> *RUTH STEBBINS THOMPSON*
> *LEON C. GRISWOLD*
> *CAROLYN RUTH GRISWOLD*
> *RUTH MARGARET WILTING*

Betty had been close to all of them. Had she not been home on furlough during the savage Tet offensive, her name might also be on the marker.

"Shadow of the Almighty" / 13

Betty shared her home with Ba Tu, a fragile, wrinkled Vietnamese lady who had served the Alliance for many years. Now, in her eighties, she was too feeble to work. Ba Tu was good company and a beloved friend.

The three eldest Mitchell children were in the States working or attending college. Sixteen-year-old Gerry attended the Alliance Dalat School, which had been moved from Vietnam to Malaysia for security reasons. Betty planned to spend Easter vacation with her youngest daughter.

The house between Betty's and the Raday church was occupied by Carolyn and John Miller and their five-year-old daughter, LuAnne. The Millers, Wycliffe Bible translators, had been living on the Alliance compound the past five months, putting the finishing touches on their Bru translation of the New Testament.

Vietnam veterans, the Millers had met at Houghton College in upstate New York where Carolyn's father was president. John, a soft-spoken country boy from a large family, had completed his education first and come to Vietnam alone. A year later, in 1960, they were married in Saigon.

The ruddy-complexioned Pennsylvania youth with his infectious laugh and his beautiful, brainy bride became very much a team. Assigned to the Bru people in northernmost South Vietnam they had lived near the war-ravaged Demilitarized Zone until the recent relocation of the Brus to a safer area near Banmethuot.

The conveniently planned, three-bedroom home was the nicest they had lived in since their marriage. Their three oldest children were attending the Wycliffe school in the coastal city of Nhatrang, so they had only their merry-eyed LuAnne for company.

On the other side of Betty's house lived an Alliance couple, Lillian and Richard Phillips. Both had a missionary heritage. Dick, a quiet, slightly built scholar had been reared in China.

Though only eleven years old when Pearl Harbor was attacked and he and his family were incarcerated by the Japanese, he had graphic memories of the eighteen-month prison experience.

Lil Amstutz, born in Khamgaon Berar, India, had come to Vietnam as a nurse and was assigned to the Dalat Clinic. Dick, who was serving in Pleiku, courted the petite blond nurse by mail. After their marriage in Dalat, they were assigned to one of the Mnong groups where there was a growing church, but no Scriptures had been translated into the dialect.

All four of the Phillips children were far off in Penang, Malaysia, at the relocated Dalat School. Lil, with a strong mother instinct, was packing with zest for their upcoming furlough, eagerly looking forward to having her family together again.

Dick was feeling the pressure to finish not only the polishing of his New Testament translation but also some revising on his doctoral thesis. He had pushed himself so hard that he was nearing the point of physical exhaustion and had twice blacked out. He had a doctor's appointment for Monday, March 10, and Lil hovered solicitously as they awaited the checkup. Dick's health was a matter of concern to all the missionaries, especially when he was not well enough to attend the regular prayer service at the Johnsons'.

The Johnsons, who lived about two blocks down the hill in the Raday village, were the newest missionaries in Banmethuot. Norman and Joan would soon complete their first term on the field. Extrovertish and outgoing, the Canadian couple were already beloved by the Raday, who kept saying they reminded them of the Ziemers.

"You look just like Bob Ziemer. You walk like him. You talk like him. Even dress like him. Surely the Lord has sent you to take his place," they were constantly telling dark-haired Norm.

And to his vivacious wife: "You are just like Marie Ziemer. You play the piano just as she did. We miss her so, we are happy you have come."

The Johnsons found it humbling to be compared to the Ziemers, but also very encouraging to find that the people remembered and loved them still. Bob Ziemer had given his life during the fateful Tet offensive, and Marie had been severely wounded and was now serving at the Alliance headquarters in Nyack, New York.

The effervescent Joan always wore a radiant smile. Like Norm, she had a great zest for life. They talked in exuberant paragraphs. Enthusiasm colored all they did, including Norm's teaching at the tribal school, Joan's nursing, and their warm, loving relationship with their two teenagers. Patricia and Doug were in Malaysia, attending school.

The new round of rumors of attack made the Johnsons, the Phillipses, and Betty Mitchell glad their children were in a place of safety. But for the Millers it was different.

"We've heard the road to Nhatrang has been closed," John told the prayer meeting group. "Before moving here, Carolyn and I decided that if for any reason that road was cut, we'd be on the next plane out. We have reservations for Tuesday. Not that we want to cause panic, but we don't want to be separated from our children should big trouble come."

The others nodded understandingly. While Malaysia would be unaffected by a sudden Communist offensive, Nhatrang might be threatened. They would feel the same way if their children were there.

For years they had faced the possibility of attack. Their mission leaders and the U.S. Embassy had outlined careful procedures in case of that eventuality. They knew every effort would be made to evacuate them if the unstable situation worsened. But they knew also that the battle had been too hot for missionaries to be evacuated during the 1968 Tet offensive.

They prayed for wisdom and courage to make the right decisions.

The next Sunday morning, March 9, following her normal routine, Betty attended church in the Raday village of Buon Aleb. As she took communion and enjoyed fellowship with her tribal brothers and sisters, she felt no special anxiety about her safety.

The Millers drove to a Bru village with two tribesmen who had been staying with them and helping to check their translation. Although a little apprehensive about the trip, they felt they should take the two Brus home before leaving for Nhatrang.

The Phillipses and the Johnsons went to the Raday church beside the compound. Three weeks before, Pastor Y Ta had begun a series of sermons based on Ephesians 5:14. He then asked Norm to preach on the same verse and Dick to do the same the following Sunday. To emphasize the text, Y Ta had hung a sign in front of the church proclaiming:

> *"Therefore it is said, 'Awake, O sleeper, and arise from the dead, and CHRIST shall give you light.'" Ephesians 5:14*

One of the Bible school students had drawn a series of pictures to illustrate the verse. The first week he pictured a Raday tribesman sleeping on his mat bed with a blanket pulled around him. The second week the picture portrayed the tribesman waking with a start when someone blew a trumpet. In the third sequence he was up and running. The pastor wanted to dramatize the need for believers to be awake and in their "armor," ready for the last days.

Day after day, Norm had prayed and meditated over the verse. But no outline came. No message jelled. Just before the services he confided to Joan, "Honey, I just can't get a message lined up. My heart is really upset, but I don't know why."

"I'll pray for you," she smiled reassuringly. "The Lord will give you what the people need."

The usually confident Norm sat nervously through the preparatory hymns and prayers, twisting the brass tribal bracelets he always wore. He still didn't know what to say when introduced. "Lord, You'll have to help me," was all he could breathe as he stepped behind the pulpit.

Opening the Raday New Testament which Bob Ziemer had helped translate, he read the assigned verse. Then because he could think of nothing more to say, he read on: *"See then that ye walk circumspectly, not as fools, but as wise, redeeming the time, because the days are evil. Wherefore be ye not unwise, but understanding what the will of the Lord is . . ."*

More Scripture came to mind. Alternately quoting, then reading, the words seemed to flow from his mouth. *"Be filled with the Spirit . . . love one another as I have loved you . . . greatly rejoice . . . that the trial of your faith . . . might be found unto praise and honor and glory . . ."* The words kept coming. Passage after passage that he had never memorized in Raday. Smoothly. Coherently. Forming a symphony of comfort and assurance. A message not from the preacher, but from the Holy Spirit to His church.

When Norm finally concluded, he felt a little breathless. He knew something unusual had happened, but wasn't quite sure why.

As they were leaving the building, a messenger arrived, panting, "Duc Loc has fallen! The NVA are on the compound of the army post there!"

And then Norm realized he had just given through the Holy Spirit a farewell message to the Raday church.

The Millers had already returned home. The Johnsons and Phillipses ran over to tell them what had happened.

"What do we do now?" John asked.

"Well, I'm going to USAID in town and ask Paul Struharick if he's heard anything," Dick announced.

Dick had just left for the AID man's house when Betty drove up. Lil quickly told her the news and asked, "What do you think we should do?"

Betty did not seem alarmed. "No sense getting too upset. I usually go by what the tribespeople say and feel. We might as well eat something, then when the witnessing groups gather at three o'clock we can ask their opinion."

Lil didn't object. Still she couldn't help but wonder if Betty would have been so calm had she been in Vietnam during Tet '68 instead of home on furlough.

Dick returned to say that Paul Struharick wasn't home. Norm and John decided they would try to find him later. In the meantime, everyone started packing a small bag, "just in case."

The Raday witnessing groups came as expected at three. But none of the tribespeople thought it safe to travel about. This made the missionaries feel something was about to happen. Then Norm and John arrived with a conflicting report.

"Paul hasn't heard anything," Norm said. "He sees no need to worry."

"But he says we can stay in the AID house if we want," John added. "His bedroom is fixed up as a bunker and we'd be safer there."

"Also, there's an extra flight to Nhatrang, leaving tomorrow," Norm continued.

"We'll be on it," Carolyn declared resolutely. "I want to be with my kids." John nodded agreement.

"Well, I don't want to leave Ba Tu," Betty exclaimed. "Who would care for her?"

"I doubt any major offensive would start with Banmethuot," Dick reasoned.

"Yeah," Norm concurred, "it would be much more logical for them to start up north. Attack Quang Tri or Danang."

"If we can just depend on our 'friends' being logical," Joan quipped.

The indecision continued throughout the afternoon. It wasn't that they were cowards; nor did anyone have a martyr complex. They just wanted to do the right thing. Finally, because Betty wouldn't leave the aged Ba Tu, the others decided they wouldn't leave Betty. They would wait for further developments. Besides, at this point there was no reason to go to the AID compound, and there were no roads open to escape from the city.

Time for evening services came and all the missionaries went to church. They could feel the tension among the tribespeople. The Raday, obviously, felt something was about to happen.

A Raday man stood to pray, then another and another until the whole church was standing, praying aloud in unison. There was no confusion or disharmony. Just a beautiful unity in the Spirit.

After church the missionaries gathered in Betty's house along with Mr. Cung, the Vietnamese missionary to the Raday, and his wife and family. Word came from the South Vietnamese military authorities that they expected an attack that night. The evening curfew had been moved from eleven o'clock to nine.

They read together the ninety-first Psalm from the Raday Bible:

"He that dwelleth in the secret place of the most High shall abide under the shadow of the Almighty. I will say of the Lord, He is my refuge and my fortress: my God; in him will I trust. Surely he shall deliver thee from the snare of the fowler, and from the noisome pestilence. . . ."

Then they joined hands and prayed, committing one another to the Lord. The missionaries felt confident in the event of an attack all stops would be pulled to evacuate them. But the Cungs would have to stay and face an uncertain future if the Communists should take over. It was hard to say goodbye to the faithful Vietnamese worker and his family.

Betty suggested the Johnsons remain on the compound and spend the night with her instead of returning to the village. "Thank you, but we'll go home," Norm said. "We left our suitcases there."

All agreed that if there was a "lot of noise" during the night, they would strike out at dawn for the USAID house. But John reminded, "If things get real bad, Paul said they might have to take us out by chopper. Maybe we'd better try to take just one bag apiece."

Betty was now admitting the possibility that Banmethuot might be attacked. After the others had gone, she looked around her house, thinking about what to take. She packed a tote bag with items that would be useful on the trail in the event of capture: soap, shampoo, toothpaste and brush, medical kit. "Lord, help me know what to select," she prayed.

Left almost undisturbed was her large green suitcase already packed for Easter vacation—things needed for civilization. She could do without her best dresses. Possessions had long lost any importance they might ever have had to her. Living in Vietnam for over two decades had given her a perspective of higher values.

The thought of leaving dear old Ba Tu behind was something else. It took all of her willpower to hold back the tears when telling the aged saint goodnight. But she found comfort in the words of the psalm that still rang in her ears: *"He shall cover thee with his feathers, and under his wings shalt thou trust: his truth shall be thy shield and buckler."*

She got together her Bible, diary, and family pictures. The thought of death or capture didn't really bother her until she looked at the pictures. There was her son, Glenn, big and broad-shouldered like his father. Because he had been born in Oregon during a furlough, he teased his sisters that he was the only one who could be president of the United States.

"Keep Glenn strong in You," Betty prayed for the one who was so much like Archie. Dependable. A good counselor. An unflagging friend. And with a touch for fixing anything mechanical. She was glad he was staying with Loretta and was close to Becki.

Loretta. Loretta, with her winsome smile, who stood so straight. Betty had to grin when she thought how many times she had fussed at all her girls, "Stand straight. Sure, you're tall. God made you that way, so stand tall and be proud of it." It had paid off; all three girls had beautiful posture.

"She's my sensitive child in many ways, Lord. She loves flowers, birds, music. Comfort her, Lord."

Becki, her firstborn. Her wedding pictures. "Thank you, Lord, that she has David." David would understand. His parents, Ruth and Ed Thompson, had died in the '68 Tet massacre. And the picture of that precious bundle, the fruit of Becki and David's love, Rachel. Betty's only grandchild. "Thank you, Lord, that I got to hold her that one day."

Betty was grateful Becki and David and Loretta and Glenn were all in San Diego. They would stick together and encourage one another.

And Gerry. Her baby. Dear, sweet child, alone in Malaysia. Not really alone, of course; she had her friends and teachers in school. They would comfort her in any way they could. Many of the school staff had known her all her life. But it wouldn't be like having her brother or sisters there.

Betty dropped to her knees by the bed. "Dear Lord, I pray

for my Gerry. I am willing to die or be captured or whatever is Your will for my life. But please, dear Jesus, be with my baby. Be especially close to her and comfort her. Give her peace. Meet all her needs.

"I pray for each of my children . . . my sisters and brothers . . . the Vietnamese people . . ." She continued on her knees, bringing the whole situation to the throne of grace, leaving it in God's hands. After a long time she crawled into bed and slept.

BOOM! The explosion shattered the silence and shook the house. Another. And another. Sirens wailed, an unnecessary notification of the attack. Betty looked at her clock. Ten minutes before three. She hurried to Ba Tu and found the elderly woman fast asleep. Her hearing was so poor even the explosions didn't wake her.

Thinking it would just be upsetting to the octogenarian to wake her, Betty let her sleep and retreated to the hallway outside Ba Tu's room. The rockets and mortars kept falling in a downpour while Betty sat on the floor to wait for the all-clear to be sounded. With the scream of each incoming missile, she prayed it wouldn't hit one of the houses. When the ground shook, there was no way to tell what had been hit.

"Thou shalt not be afraid for the terror by night," came the reassurance from Scripture.

Next door Dick and Lil were squeezed into a tiny, coffin-sized closet off an interior hallway. It was the safest place in the cement and brick house. Their faithful German shepherd, Gretchen, whined in fear from her hidingplace under a bed.

At each near miss Dick and Lil instinctively pulled up their feet and covered their faces. They knew a direct hit would bring instant death, but a glancing blow might only wound them. They wanted to be able to run and to see. They, too, thought of the psalm. *"A thousand shall fall at thy side, and ten thousand at thy right hand; but it shall not come nigh thee,"* Lil murmured.

Little LuAnne Miller hadn't even been awakened by the bombardment, perhaps because she had heard the sounds of war since she was a baby. John carried her, still sleeping, into the windowless hallway where the three snuggled together for protection.

"Because thou hast made the Lord, which is my refuge, even the most High, thy habitation; there shall no evil befall thee." The psalm continued to comfort the Millers also.

John and Carolyn couldn't count the number of nights they had spent under fire. But at Tet '68 they had been apart. Carolyn and the children were with the Phillipses and other colleagues at a translation workshop in Kontum. John had been in Danang where he knew only that Kontum was under attack. No missionary adult or child had been hurt at Kontum while a bloody battle raged just outside their bunker. But John had not known this until after they were evacuated.

Four A.M. The bombardment continued. Five. No letup in the pounding. The missionaries in the compound houses anxiously awaited dawn, when they expected the "noise" to stop. Except for the dreadful Tet, seven years before, it had always happened that way.

At last the first streaks of light slipped through the windows. The pounding stopped, but only to give way to more terrifying sounds. The shouts of foot soldiers, the crackle of small arms fire, and the rumble of Communist tanks.

Carolyn had already pulled on two pairs of black pants and buttoned up two shirts as a contingency in case of capture. Now she and John were scraping up linguistic notebooks, files, their precious Bru unpublished translation of the New Testament, and other manuscripts and throwing them in their Land Rover. All indecision was past. They would try to make the USAID compound in a last-ditch attempt to escape.

The Phillipses also knew there were only minutes to spare. While Dick bundled up his priceless Mnong manuscripts, Lil got the negatives of pictures of their children taken during the past term in Vietnam.

Betty had a visitor, Pastor Y Ta, who had run from his house as bullets whizzed about. "Go now, *Aduon*," he begged. "Go!"

"But what about Ba Tu?" Betty protested.

"I'll care for her," the pastor insisted. "Hurry. Go, before it is too late."

Everyone converged on the Millers' Land Rover, tossing bags and translation materials in unceremoniously. Betty tossed in her green suitcase. "What about Norm and Joan?" she asked.

"We can't go down there," John declared. "We'll all be trapped."

Dick agreed sadly, adding hopefully, "They may have left already."

"Go on!" Y Ta pressed. "I'll send word you are going to the USAID house and to follow if they can."

Betty hastily handed the keys to her house and car to the pastor. Dick dashed back inside his house and returned dragging the frightened shepherd, Gretchen. "She doesn't want to come. But it's better for her to be outside than left in to starve."

As John spun the starter, Betty called to Y Ta, "Take any of my things you can use."

Dick, looking very pale, pressed against Lil. With everyone bent low and Carolyn protecting LuAnne with her own body, John took off with a roar.

They screeched around the corner of the side road and onto Highway 14 on two wheels. Betty took one last glance at the road leading down to the Johnsons in hopes of seeing them or their jeep. The street was empty.

Graveside service for missionaries killed in the 1968 Tet offensive at Banmethuot.

Memorial to the six Alliance missionaries killed at Banmethuot in the 1968 Communist Tet offensive.
Photo by James C. Hefley

Sample of destruction of missionary homes during 1968 Tet battle.
Photo by James C. Hefley

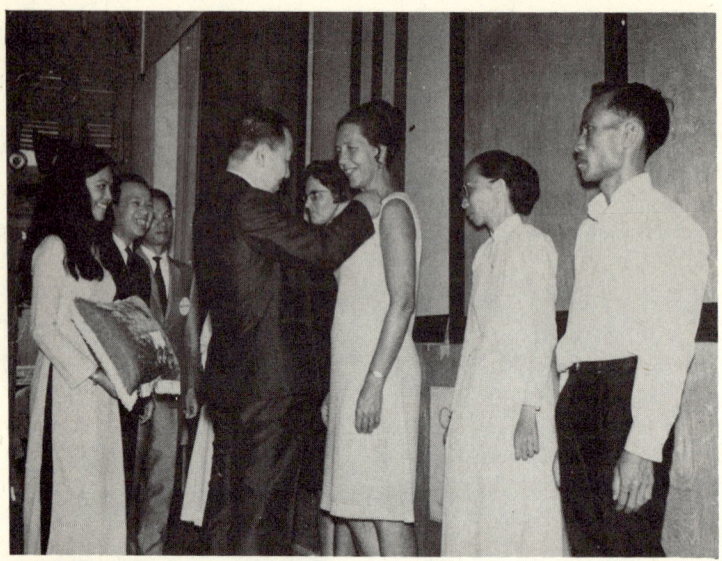

Betty Mitchell receives award in South Vietnam. (Below) The Norman Johnson family in South Vietnam setting.

John and Carolyn Miller while working among the Bru people in the northern region of South Vietnam.

Betty Mitchell and witness team.

Johnnie Phillips watches his mother at work in Banmethuot. This picture represents many hours of typing portions of Scripture, literacy primers, and other literature in the Mnong language.

2

"Act Like Prisoners"

John, driving at full speed, caught glimpses of startled expressions from soldiers staring at the vehicle full of pale-faced foreigners careening down the streets through the battle. He slammed to a halt at the entrance of the USAID compound and they waited impatiently for the Raday guard to unlock and open the gates. Then they drove into the courtyard, grabbed whatever hand luggage they could while the gates were being locked behind them, and ran.

Paul Struharick, the blond agricultural adviser for Darlac Province, met them at the door of the two-story house. "Where are the Johnsons?" he asked as they hurried into the hallway.

"We were hoping they would already be here," John replied.

"Not yet."

"We sent them a message that we were coming."

The USAID man nodded approval. "Then they should be here soon. Come on upstairs."

The group followed him up to the living room area. The house was laid out so that the bedrooms were downstairs in the safest place, while the kitchen and living areas were above. A short, dark, broad-shouldered man rose to be introduced as they entered the room.

"Meet Peter Whitlock. He flew in from Saigon yesterday."

"Great timing, what?" Peter said cryptically in his broad Australian accent while shaking hands all around.

"Have you had radio contact with anyone?" Dick asked.

"Well, with the electricity off I can't use my big sets," Paul explained. "All I have is this little battery-operated one," he said, indicating the small apparatus in his hand.

"From what I heard from the local station this is a massive offensive. Looks as if our only hope of getting out is by helicopter. At least this unit is strong enough to have contact with a plane or chopper."

Paul left to climb more stairs leading to the roof where he had stationed some of his Vietnamese USAID employees as lookouts. There was a good deal of running up and down stairs and milling about. No one seemed certain of what was happening or what they should do.

Shortly after the missionaries settled down they were joined by another American, a tall, thin, unkempt-looking young man carrying a flight bag. Jay Scarborough said he was in Vietnam on a Ford Foundation grant to photograph some ancient Cham manuscripts. He, too, had been on the last flight into Banmethuot.

"Wouldn't you know that one was on schedule," he remarked sarcastically.

The missionaries were getting more and more concerned about the Johnsons. "Don't you think I ought to go check on them?" John asked Paul.

"Let's give them a little more time," Paul advised. "They should be here soon."

By eight o'clock John was getting fidgety. "I really think I ought to go."

"I'm afraid it's too late now," Paul announced, grim-faced. "I just got a report of heavy fighting between here and the Johnsons' house. Looks as if you got out just in time."

Stunned, the missionaries sat in silence as the sounds of battle grew ominously louder. They hoped the Johnsons had made it to a neighbor's bunker in time.

Paul called his employees together and told them they could go home if they chose, or they were welcome to stay. Ike Tolontino, a Filipino, decided to remain, as did the two Raday guards and a young Vietnamese man with his wife and little son and sister-in-law.

"I think we'd better go down into my bedroom," Paul declared. "The walls have iron reinforcements so it serves as a bunker. We'll be a lot safer there."

With heavy artillery pounding in their ears, they crowded downstairs into the fifteen-by-fifteen-foot room. Dick was so woozy that Lil insisted he stretch out on the bed. Others sat around on the floor. Jay nervously paced up and down. Paul suggested that since they might have to stay cloistered in that room for some time it would be better for smokers to step into the hall rather than contaminate the air.

They heard tanks rumbling along the asphalt street in front of the house. "Our best bet is to be as quiet as possible so that our 'friends' won't know anyone is in here," Paul whispered. Everyone complied.

Betty leaned against a wall, trying to get as comfortable as possible. As her eyes adjusted to the darkened room she looked around at the others. Noticing how close the other women stayed to their husbands, she felt very lonely. If only Archie were with her, the situation wouldn't seem so bad. She consoled herself with the thought that if they were captured, perhaps they would be taken to the same prison camp where Archie was being held. Could this be the Lord's way of reuniting them?

The rumble of the tanks and the continual firing of bullets interspersed with an occasional explosion of a hand grenade covered the subdued whispering of Carolyn trying to explain to LuAnne the necessity for being quiet. She pulled a puzzle from her overnight bag and the fair-skinned, blond youngster was soon sitting on the floor happily putting the pieces together.

Time dragged by and Betty looked down at her blue-faced Timex. It was difficult to see in the gloomy room. The only light came from the door open to the interior hallway. As best she could make out it was past noon.

A foray was made upstairs to the kitchen where food was quickly prepared and brought back down into the bunker. "We'll have to go easy on the chow," Paul said apologetically. "We may have to be here for a while."

The sound of running footsteps outside the house increased the stress they felt. Even the children sensed the tension and remained quiet. The rumbling on the street continued, and Betty remembered that the tribespeople had told her a week before that the jungle was full of tanks. They had not exaggerated.

Midafternoon squawks from Paul's radio announced the presence of a USAID plane overhead. Paul stepped into the hallway where the chance of his voice being heard outside was less. When he returned, his drooping head and stooped shoulders indicated his discouragement.

"I'm afraid the news isn't good. There is too much enemy antiaircraft to even consider landing a chopper. Apparently our hopes of being evacuated are about nil. We'll just have to stay quiet and hope we aren't discovered until the battle is over. If they found us now, they would probably come in shooting. After things have calmed down we might be able to surrender peacefully."

The group sat speechless. Their future possibilities seemed limited to death or capture.

"I was able to report our names, so our relatives can be informed of our presence here. I also told them about the Johnsons, and they said they would fly over that area in hopes of spotting something. They'll fly back over in an hour for another sked."

"At least our children will know we're alive," Betty murmured. The others nodded agreement.

The long hours of silence that followed gave the missionaries time to think. Of their position, of their loved ones, of the future for the Vietnamese Christians. They wondered if the Alliance compound had been destroyed again and if the Raday church had been blown apart. And most of all, if the Johnsons were still alive.

The hourly skeds with the plane brought no news, only confirmation that this was indeed a massive attack that would not easily be repulsed.

They maintained silence as much as possible, fearing to even flush the toilet lest the noise be detected by passing soldiers. By nightfall the bathroom, just off the bedroom, had become so odious that occasionally when a mortar went off nearby someone would chance pulling the handle in unison with the explosion.

The flickering flame of one small candle set in the middle of the floor was the only light they dared use during that long dark night. Finding a comfortable position to sleep in the crowded room was difficult, but the uncertainty of the future precluded much slumber anyway. It was a time to think and to pray.

Betty was concerned about the Johnsons. They had become

34 / Prisoners of Hope

a vital part of the missionary team in Banmethuot so quickly. Was it their zeal and enthusiasm? Or their open, accepting friendliness? Betty considered this awhile.

No, she finally concluded. The tie she felt with the Johnsons was the same as with all the missionaries: common commitment. A dual commitment to Christ and to the people of Vietnam. This had moved Norm to give up his career as a teacher, and Joan hers as a nurse. They had sold their split-level home, furniture, and car and uprooted their two children because of their commitment to Christ.

And that was why all of them were there. Because their love for Christ constrained them to follow Him. Betty ran back over her own years in Vietnam. They hadn't been easy, but then Christ had never promised that following Him would be easy.

She remembered her final interview before being accepted as a missionary. As a young bride-to-be she had been asked if her commitment was strong enough to endure possible separation from her husband. She quickly responded, "Yes," never dreaming how long a separation she would be called upon to endure.

But as she reviewed her life she knew that she would give the same reply today. If she had her life to live over, she would change nothing, for her life was Christ's and she could but live it as He directed. That must have been what Jesus meant when He said, "Lose your life and you will find it." Without a commitment so strong you were willing to die for it, life wasn't really worth living anyway, she concluded.

Her children were old enough and mature enough in the Lord to understand this. She knew that, though it would hurt them deeply, they would be willing to give her up, if necessary, since they, too, had resolved to serve God, accepting His will in all things.

The Phillipses didn't have this assurance, for their children were much younger. Jean was only thirteen. Such a vulnerable

"Act Like Prisoners" / 35

age, and yet as the oldest she seemed to show responsibility toward her younger brothers and sister. Brian was eleven and Ruthie had just had her ninth birthday. And Johnnie was only six. It was his first year away from his parents.

But it was comforting to Dick and Lil to know they were safe at school in Malaysia. What if the attack had come during vacation when they had all been home? They knew that the staff at the Dalat School would give their children the best of loving care. And if they should be killed, Lil's brother had agreed to raise the children for them. They had been committed to the Lord at birth, there was nothing more they could do for them now.

It was more difficult for the Millers, for their children were in Nhatrang. Would this "massive offensive" reach that far? Could North Vietnamese strategy be to cut the country in two? Would there be time to evacuate the children to Saigon? Huddled in the dark room, John and Carolyn tried not to dwell on such questions.

Their children, also born during the turbulent sixties, were close in age to the Phillips children. Marjorie was twelve, Gordon ten, and Nathan seven. John and Carolyn knew that the Wycliffe houseparents at Nhatrang, Nancy and Jim Cooper, would protect the children as if they were their own. Surely at the first harbinger of impending danger the school would be moved from its location on the South China Sea to safety. But it was hard to be separated from them during a time of danger.

And there was LuAnne. Sleeping the peaceful slumber of childhood. The sounds of war were too familiar to her young ears to keep her awake. The soft, rhythmic breathing evidenced her complete trust and confidence in her parents. She wasn't afraid as long as she had her mommy and daddy.

There were no reports from the airplane during the night hours, but the group huddled in the bedroom/bunker could hear the determined battle the South Vietnamese were making to defend Banmethuot. From all the "noise" it seemed the North Vietnamese army was just as determined to capture it. They had no way of knowing which side was winning.

While they waited in uncertainty through the long frightful night, the missionaries whispered quotes from the psalm which had comforted them the night before.

At last, dawn. But the coming of daylight brought neither peace nor quiet. How long would the battle continue? Would the whole city be destroyed? Reports from the USAID plane were not encouraging. They settled in for another day of waiting.

Through whispered encounters the missionaries learned that Peter Whitlock was with the Australian Broadcasting Commission on loan to the government of Thailand. He had been in Saigon checking literacy programs for tribal people, looking for ideas that might be useful in Thailand. He had flown to Banmethuot to study the literacy work of the missionaries and to visit the local radio station, which broadcast in tribal languages. He was to return Tuesday on the same plane the Millers had intended to take out. "But I rather doubt the transportation system will be functioning properly today," he sighed.

Coming to Vietnam the first time with the International Voluntary Service, Jay Scarborough had taught English in Phan Rang where there was a large percentage of Cham tribespeople. There he had met the Dave Bloods and had become acquainted with the work of the Wycliffe Bible Translators.

Returning to the States, he enrolled in law school, then took a semester off when the grant came to photograph the ancient Cham manuscripts in Vietnam. While working on that project, his film loader was stolen. Figuring it would take a week to get a new one from the States, he decided to take time to visit former students attending the Banmethuot Normal School. "That was the whimsy of fate which brought me here at this time," he said sardonically.

"Act Like Prisoners" / 37

While Peter and Jay cursed their misfortune at having come at the wrong time, Paul was thankful the attack had not been delayed another week, because his Raday wife and child were expected in from Bangkok in a few days.

The children were restless, and it was becoming more difficult to keep them quiet. The adults, too, were getting a little stir-crazy. From time to time some of the men would walk around in the hallway, but the continual sounds of battle outside kept anyone from getting ideas about leaving the building.

At intervals they heard footsteps in the street; as they came closer everyone would hold their breath, wondering if they would be discovered. But the day wore on without any attempt at entry.

John's beard was getting itchy so he, and then Dick, tried a "noiseless" shave. A bath would have felt great, but it would have been foolish to run that much water.

The waiting was nervewracking. Lil recalled Vange Blood telling of how at Tet '68 the troops had thrown in grenades before storming into their house. The thought of the havoc such an explosion would cause in the midst of their overpopulated hideout made Lil shiver. Surely the battle would be over soon.

Paul Struharick fashioned a white flag from a pillowcase and set it outside the bedroom door for the time when, inevitably, they would be found. Since Paul spoke Raday, but little Vietnamese, it was decided that Jay, who had a good command of the national language, should accompany him outside if soldiers began a forced entry into the courtyard.

The perception of time became warped as day faded into a second night. It seemed they had been shut in that room for weeks. All they could do was wait. Just wait.

Another dawn. Wednesday, March 12. The tension of waiting, not knowing what was happening or what the future would bring was telling on everyone. Little irritations flared out of

38 / Prisoners of Hope

proportion. The children were tired of being quiet. They were all feeling grimy. And still the battle raged.

Then, shortly after noon, came the noise they had been dreading: the sawing of the lock in the gate. Paul took a deep breath and picked up his white flag. Jay was right behind him.

As they started out the door John realized it was nearly time to talk with the plane again. "Shall we try to keep the sked?" he asked.

"No," Peter responded resolutely, "it's too dangerous. Don't try it."

Ike quickly changed the little radio's frequency then tossed it back on the bed. They heard the outside door close behind Paul and Jay.

The group inside remained in absolute, motionless silence. Hearts beat fast, muscles knotted, and ears strained for some indication of what was happening in the courtyard. It hurt even to breathe.

Lil, standing next to the bed, felt her knees turning to rubber as she started shaking. Dick put an unsteady arm around his wife. Carolyn and John clutched LuAnne tightly between them, trying to shield her from whatever was about to happen. "God help us all," Betty whispered.

"Come out with your hands raised," came the command in Vietnamese. "Come one at a time." They lined up single file and slowly, falteringly obeyed.

"Take off your glasses," one of the North Vietnamese soldiers instructed Dick and Lil as they passed him. They looked at his Russian-made rifle and complied. As they entered the courtyard they asked another guard if they could put their glasses back on and he gave permission. The invaders seemed surprised to find such a collection of foreigners and apparently didn't know what to do with them.

Several NVA troops entered the house and started running around, smashing things, checking for any possible hideouts.

The breaking of glass and wood inside the house did nothing to calm the fears of the motley group crowded together in the courtyard.

When the captives were instructed to line up along the street, then to sit down and wait, they quickly obeyed, noting that their guards were nervous and excited.

While sitting there waiting to learn their fate Betty opened the Bible she had carried out with her and found a program the young people had prepared for their coming conference. Their theme verse, Philippians 2:15, seemed to leap out at her: *That ye may be blameless and harmless, the sons of God, without rebuke, in the midst of a crooked and perverse nation, among whom ye shine as lights in the world.*

"Praise the Lord!" she said to herself. "That's exactly what I want my life to be—a light to those who sit in darkness." But even as she prayed, claiming that verse, it seemed the Lord said to her, "But you must take the verse that comes before, too." She looked at verse 14: *"Do all things without murmurings and disputings."*

"Very well, Lord," she promised. "I'll do my best not to complain no matter what happens. Just please use me for Your glory in the days to come."

"Who are you?" The demanding voice snapped her to attention. "What is your name? And your birthplace?"

"I am Betty Mitchell. I was born in the United States."

"What business have you here? And what is your rank?"

"I'm here on God's business, and I have no rank. I'm just a missionary."

"Show me some identification."

Each of the captives was asked for the same information.

When the NVA were satisfied nothing in the house could be used against them they allowed some of the prisoners to go back for their belongings. The Phillipses and the Millers got their bags containing the manuscripts. John passed over a suitcase that contained a radio and tape recorder, thinking these items might be construed as subversive, and instead picked up an old Wesson Oil bottle they had used for a water jug.

"Where are the keys to the vehicles?" commanded a rather jittery officer. John and Paul fished out their keys and handed them over. "You will be taken from here," they were informed by the officer who seemed quite anxious to be rid of them. The Asians and non-Asians were separated. "Get in this one," he ordered the pale-faced foreigners, gesturing toward a familiar Land Rover.

The missionaries exchanged significant looks, but said nothing. They were being put in the Millers' Land Rover, which had most of their belongings in the back. A young Vietnamese in plain clothes got behind the wheel. Another climbed in behind the five missionaries. Paul, Peter, and Jay then squeezed in among them.

As they bounced along the road leading out of the city Lil eyed the long thin hand rocket the young guard kept pointing in her direction.

"Where is your homeland?" she asked him in Vietnamese.

"Hanoi," he responded.

Because he didn't seem belligerent, she asked him to please point the rocket away from the passengers, and he complied. But when he was asked where they were going he shook his head and lapsed into silence. The ride didn't last long. They were soon unloaded at a coffee plantation being used as a clearing station for prisoners being taken in the battle.

They were lined up and any possessions that seemed to have military significance were taken from them. That included radios, cameras, tape recorders, and, unfortunately, the Phillipses' negatives. Lil hated to surrender all those precious reminders of her children's growing-up years, but she did so without complaint.

The soldiers made a ring around the prisoners while the

"Act Like Prisoners" / 41

superiors discussed their future. LuAnne, hiding behind her mother, peeked out with big, blue eyes, inspecting all the green-clad men with their long rifles. Finally she looked up at Carolyn and asked, "Mommy, are these soldiers here to protect us from the Communists?"

Carolyn hesitated a moment and then answered, "No, Honey, they are the Communists."

But the guards didn't look particularly menacing. Most appeared to be only in their late teens. So the prisoners began talking to them. They found most were from near Hanoi. One was married and the father of a new baby. They seemed no different from other Vietnamese the missionaries had known and loved over the years.

Overwhelmed at the relief of being out of immediate danger and refreshed by being out in the sunshine and out of the gloom of the bunker, the missionaries tended to overreact. Those who could speak Vietnamese chatted amiably with the guards. Betty and Lil teased in Raday and laughed out loud about something. It was so good to laugh again that they giggled more than was wise. One of the officers stalked over to the group, obviously furious.

"Stop this!" he shouted. "You will act like prisoners. You will not talk to the guards."

He stormed away and the prisoners sat down and talked among themselves, thankful to break the silence of the bunker and to be away from the midst of battle. They continued to relax, and, again, enjoyed themselves a little too much.

The officer stalked back, incensed. "You are not behaving like prisoners. You must not talk so much. And if you must talk, use only Vietnamese!" he barked.

Then the prisoners understood the problem: the officer couldn't understand what they were saying and thought they might be laughing at their captors.

"But we don't all speak Vietnamese," Dick protested.

"And what about LuAnne?" John added. "She doesn't understand any Vietnamese. We have to be able to talk to her."

The officer peered at the bright-eyed child who looked back at him with childish innocence. "Well," he relented, "don't talk so much."

The group huddled closer together and conversed quietly among themselves, but the curiosity of the guards overcame their discipline and as soon as the officer was out of hearing range, they resumed talking to the foreigners.

The missionaries' main anxiety at this time was their uncertain status. Were they being held as prisoners of war or merely being detained as refugees until they could be evacuated? Their situation was too insecure to risk asking questions. They were also deeply concerned about Joan and Norm Johnson and spent most of the afternoon scanning the faces of approaching newcomers. If all prisoners from Banmethuot were being brought here, then Norm and Joan should be arriving soon. Unless . . .

Toward evening LuAnne, who had been so good during the past anxious three days, started crying. "I'm hungry," she wailed to her mother. It had been a long time since they'd had anything to eat.

The guards asked why the little girl was crying and after learning the problem managed to come up with some *luong kho,* a dried protein wafer. It was very nourishing, but had to be washed down with water. LuAnne was satisfied.

Soon all prisoners were given some rations. The fare was not the tastiest but they were grateful to get it. They continued sitting on the hard ground as the evening wore on, wondering what was going to happen. When would they know?

When darkness fell they were instructed to get back into the Land Rover; they were to be taken further from the scene of battle. They got up, stretched, gathered the few possessions they had with them, and straggled back to the vehicle. The officer seemed displeased with their lack of military discipline, but they were cooperating so he said nothing.

As they climbed into the Rover Lil positioned herself on one of the two small, facing back seats. On the short trip to the plantation her right leg had become very cramped. Because she had previously suffered from phlebitis, she feared a long ride would aggravate her poor circulation and swelling and perhaps another clot might result.

She was arranging some of the baggage so that she could sit with her leg raised when the head guard came behind the Rover and ordered her out. "You sit in the front," he told her and ordered a guard to take her place. Lil wasn't sure why they had been rearranged, but she thanked the Lord for having room to stretch out her legs.

Carolyn sat directly behind the driver with LuAnne on her lap and John, Betty, Dick, Peter, Paul, Jay, and the guard squeezed in surrounded with all the paraphernalia. The space seemed even smaller when they were instructed to close all the windows because the trail was narrow and branches might snap in their faces.

"What power! Zzrrooom!" the driver voiced his delight, sensing the power of the Rover as they lurched into the dark jungle. They followed what was supposed to be a logging road, but it was little more than a path. Twisting, turning, often stopping and backing around an obstacle, they bounced toward an unknown destination. Occasionally a plane was heard overhead and the driver would turn out the lights, taking no chance of alerting enemy aircraft.

They came to a stream where a detail of soldiers had been charged with setting logs in place for vehicles to cross. Each vehicle, of course, forced the logs out of position, and the soldiers would sit and wait until they were needed again. It was the first of a number of such crews they came upon during their trip.

At each crossing, the "loggers" gathered around the Land Rover. Some became very loud and boisterous, angry at the pale-faced foreigners they presumed were the cause of all the war and misery they had endured.

"Be careful," the guard next to Lil would order each new crew. "We have women in here and a child, too. Be calm." These guards were protecting them from other Communists. What kind of treatment could they expect in a prison camp?

After three or four hours they were dumped with all their belongings at a jungle campsite.

"Hey, I don't want all this stuff," John protested when the guards began unloading all the equipment he regularly kept in the back of the Land Rover.

"Do these things belong to you?" he was asked.

"Well, yes," he admitted with a shrug, "but we don't need all that out here in the jungle. Just leave it in the Rover."

"We were told to leave you and your possessions at this place," was the reply. There was no point in protesting further. So the Millers were stuck with carrying along a couple of tennis rackets, typewriter, sewing machine, a set of melmac dishes, and cooking utensils, along with various other nonessentials.

They were led to a makeshift office containing a desk with a candle on it and little else. After their names and identification were taken, they were led to an area in the clearing and told this was where they would spend the night.

Completely exhausted, they felt they could sleep anywhere. The only problem was mosquitoes. Fortunately, the Millers had a net in their collection. They spread it over a suitcase. LuAnne wriggled under the net and used the luggage as a bed. The rest spread out clockwise around her, inching their heads under the net and covering their bodies with whatever was available. Thus they spent their first night sleeping under the stars.

Dr. Phillips points to an illustration as Pastor M. Brong looks on in basic doctrinal class in Mnong short-term Bible school.

Betty Mitchell gives the "Bread of Life" to hungry Vietnamese. (Below) Carolyn and John Miller share a laugh with Bru translation assistants at Wycliffe Translation Center in Nhatrang, Vietnam.
Photo by Hugh Steven

3

Grit, Grime, and Grace

The prisoners awoke the next morning to discover they were camped by a cool, flowing stream shaded by bamboo. Breakfast consisted of more *luong kho* and water. John pulled out his little pocket calendar and checked off another day. March 13. What would this day bring?

Hundreds of Vietnamese and tribal people were milling around the small clearing. Prisoners and their guards. The men were made to take off their shoes and place them in a big pile to discourage an attempted escape.

One of the most private areas of life for North Americans suddenly became very public. Three totally inadequate holes that constituted the sanitary facilities of the camp could in no way service so many people. The women held off the call of nature for as long as possible, then went together to the latrine area where each would take a turn while the other two held up Betty's Raday skirt as a shield from view. The guards politely turned their backs, but the women were humiliated by the total lack of privacy.

They returned to find the men discussing their location. "I think we're near Buon Ky," Dick surmised. Dick still felt woozy, but he had kept a clear head. "We were heading north during the night, and this stream looks familiar." They talked with some of the other prisoners and concluded that was where they were. For some reason it was comforting to have some idea of their location.

They sat around watching the comings and goings of the other prisoners, looking for people they knew. Especially Joan and Norm Johnson. Betty spotted a Raday preacher, still wearing his white Sunday suit. At first he turned his head, pretending he didn't know them. Not wanting to cause him any trouble, the missionaries ignored him. But soon he overcame his fear and came and talked to them. He had been captured on his way home from church four days before.

The Millers saw a Mnong boy they knew well. Others talked to them as the hours dragged on. "You'll be set free soon," the national prisoners agreed. "When you are free will you tell my wife I am alive?" a sad-eyed man asked, passing a note. A number of other messages and notes were given the missionaries. They wished they could be as certain of an early release.

The next day they were moved a little nearer the stream where they had more privacy. Since there were more and more prisoners arriving and the *bo doi* (guards) were having difficulty keeping enough water boiled, the foreigners volunteered to boil their own water supply. They were issued an empty *luong kho* tin for this purpose and set about making their own fire, being careful to observe the warnings about producing too much smoke.

Twice a day they were issued more rice than they could eat.

"Maybe we'd better force ourselves to eat more," Dick proposed. "Rations might not be good for long."

They had adjusted to their sleeping arrangements and had discovered they were really quite adept at improvising. A tribal skirt laid flat could be either a mat for sleeping upon or a covering. Sleeping in their clothes made it less necessary to have much bedding, though it did get quite nippy after the sun went down.

Betty felt especially thankful that the large green suitcase she had packed for her Easter vacation had been left in the Millers' Land Rover. It contained many useful items including a pillow which she let LuAnne use. She had carried another pillow out of the bunker with her. A real luxury, it was covered in pink satin with a scooped-out section to fit around her neck to keep her fancy upswept hairdo nice.

She certainly didn't feel fancy now; it had been nearly a week since she'd had a bath. But the pillow did make sleeping on the hard ground more endurable.

On the fifteenth they were delighted to be reunited with a foot-weary Ike Tolontino. "Finally they decided I was a foreigner, too," the Filipino explained, "so I get to stay with you guys. I only wish I had gotten to ride like you," he moaned, rubbing his weary, blistered feet.

"What do you call this place?" he asked.

"Oh, this is the Rose Garden," Dick quipped. They all convulsed in laughter. The primitive sanitary conditions had caused a ripe stench that would have made "The Sewer" a more appropriate name.

That day all the foreigners were instructed to write several papers giving biographical information. They spent some time getting the dozen or so questions answered to the best of their ability, but after they turned them in an officer came to Lil and complained, "You have this wrong."

He pointed to the question, Why are you here? She had replied, "Because I was captured by the North Vietnamese."

"You must say you were captured by the Provisional Revolutionary Government or by the National Liberation Front. You were not captured by the North Vietnamese." His accent so obviously marked him as a northerner that his request was ludicrous. Despite his speech, and the accents of most of their guards, there was no smiling. Lil solemnly redid the paper to his satisfaction.

Until this time only Paul Struharick, as an official of the United States Agency for International Development, and thus an employee of the State Department, had been given any special attention. Now Betty took the opportunity to ask if there was any information available about her husband.

Despite the fact that she had told of Archie's capture on her information sheet, the officer looked puzzled. "How do you expect me to know about him?" he replied, marching off in a huff.

Later the bedraggled foreigners were assembled for group pictures. Then Paul was pulled out and directed to stand at the front of a group of Vietnamese prisoners, with the photographer zeroing in on his bronze tribal bracelet. They could only speculate what propaganda use that would serve.

After supper that night they were informed they would be moving to another camp. They had no particular affection for the Rose Garden, but leaving without having seen the Johnsons seemed rather ominous.

They turned in their rice bowls, gathered up their belongings, and walked over to the truck in which they were to ride. It was a large GMC that had been "liberated" from the South Vietnamese.

"If anyone has anything that in any way might upset the officials at a real prison camp, I suggest they dispose of it now," Paul said softly.

"I have a note one of the prisoners gave me for his wife," Lil remembered.

"Get rid of it," Paul ordered. "It might endanger every one of us."

Flustered, Lil looked around for some place she could drop the offending piece of paper. If it were found on the ground, she felt it might cause trouble for the man who had written it. She crumpled it in her hand and then popped it in her mouth. After she had chewed it sufficiently so that the message was indecipherable, she spit it out.

Guards came and began tying them together, one left arm to the next person's right arm, in groups of ten. The foreigners climbed into the back of the truck with a group of South Vietnamese army officers. The twenty of them filled the truck, but another ten were added. In the jam Lil became concerned about her leg. Carolyn worried about LuAnne and snuggled her little daughter close. Now came the command for ten more to squeeze in. The crush became so great that no one could turn. With bodies jammed together it was hard even to breathe. They could only hope the trip wouldn't last long.

When the truck moved downhill the bodies slid forward in a mass. If they tried to hold on to one of the slats in the sides of the truck a guard would shine a light and bark, "Take your hands off!"

When they started up a hill, the tilting of the truck bed caused everyone to slide toward the tail gate. With no time to rearrange themselves as they started downhill, they all slid toward the cab. Any sharp curve caused another shift of bodies.

Because they were tied together, the sheer press of their numbers made it impossible to get repositioned. LuAnne huddled against her mother, but whenever they started sliding Carolyn would try frantically to protect her little girl, fearful that the child literally would be crushed.

52 / Prisoners of Hope

The truck rolled on and on. Hour after miserable, endless hour. They stopped once at a river and water was passed around, but no one was allowed to get out. Then off again with no idea of how much longer they would have to endure being squashed together. Many of the passengers were becoming nauseous, but there was no stopping.

Finally, after over seven hours they arrived. "Get out!" a voice shouted. After being cramped for so long it was not an easy command to obey, but somehow they managed.

They were met by the camp political leader. The little Vietnamese officer was "smiling," but his look was more like a sneer or a smirk. He "welcomed" them, with Jay interpreting for those who didn't speak Vietnamese. They were then led a short way to their sleeping quarters—a pile of thatch scattered across the ground.

Too exhausted to think of bugs or snakes or other possible inhabitants of the thatch, they got their heads under the Millers' mosquito net and fell asleep almost instantly.

All too soon the clanging of a gong jolted them. It wasn't really much of a gong, just a pan lid banged upon with a metal spoon, but it did the job. As they rolled out of the hay, literally, they noticed that during the night they had been marched into a stockade. A bamboo fence made of six-foot poles stuck vertically into the ground and held together by a few horizontal sticks defined the perimeter of their area. The flimsy structure would not have kept anyone in who was determined to leave, but the well-armed guards prevented anyone from getting ideas.

"And we used to think Jungle Camp was primitive," John moaned.

"Yeah," Carolyn agreed. "Wycliffe has a training camp for primitive living in southern Mexico where recruits are taught to survive in uncivilized areas," she explained to the others. "Compared to this that was pure luxury."

Grit, Grime and Grace / 53

"This is basic living all right," Betty concurred, looking around at the wall-less, floorless huts into which the other prisoners were jammed. "But the worst thing about it is not knowing how long we'll be here."

The new prisoners were issued white plastic bowls with their morning rice, which they ate with bamboo chopsticks the men had whittled back at the Rose Garden. When they finished their meal they had no water to wash their utensils, so they licked them clean. John rebelled against that demeaning method of cleaning and instead poured a little hot water in his bowl, swished it around, and drank it.

Reflecting on this, he realized his method wasn't all that superior. "I never thought I'd drink dishwater," he lamented with a wry grin.

In their grim surroundings any attempt at humor was appreciated, and he was rewarded with a round of ironic chuckles.

As more prisoners kept arriving, more thatch-roofed huts went up. Apparently this was intended to be a large camp. Even the thatch the foreigners had slept on was used to make a shelter for them.

Paul became the natural leader of the group—a position he refused to consider officially. He walked off the size of the new facility. "About nine by twelve feet. Sure not much space for ten foreigners." Then he checked the roof. "That might protect us from the sunshine, but it'll never keep out the rain," the USAID man predicted.

"Well, we could just call this Camp Sunshine," Carolyn suggested with a forced grin.

This was their first Sunday in captivity. It was difficult for the missionaries to realize that only one week before they had been with their tribal friends worshiping in peace. It seemed a lifetime ago. John pulled out his Bible and settled down to read. One of the guards came over and rattled off some instructions to him that he didn't catch.

"He says you can't read that," Jay translated for him.

John opened his mouth to disagree, thought better of it, and closed his Bible. The missionaries looked at one another questioningly. Did this mean they would be deprived of the reassurance of God's Word during their captivity?

Because of Jay's fluency in Vietnamese, he had become the group's unofficial translator. Later that afternoon they realized he was in for another round of translating when he announced, "Don't look now, but here comes 'Happy.' " Sure enough the camp political officer, still wearing his smirky grin, was approaching.

He began reciting in a dull monotone, "It is my privilege to tell you of the glories of our revolution. It is a revolution that shall surely be victorious, even as your American revolution was. Because our cause is just. The just cause always wins.

"We want to inform you prisoners that even though our country has been the victim of many crimes perpetrated by the United States government, we do not hold you personally responsible. The American people are not our enemy, only the American government.

"Our revolution gives fair treatment to all prisoners who cooperate. If you have proper attitudes, cooperate with all camp officials, and obey all the rules, you will be treated well.

"We desire true freedom for all people," he continued, prefacing a long discourse on the purpose of their "glorious revolution."

"If it is true that you bring freedom, does that include freedom of religion?" John asked.

"Of course. Our people have freedom of religion," Happy simpered.

"Then why did the guard forbid me to read my Bible?"

Happy's face darkened perceptibly. He turned and spoke quietly to the guard a moment, then turned back to John. "We have religious freedom," he insisted. "You may read whatever you want." He then turned on his heels and left.

Shortly afterward the group was issued individual tarps; actually just khaki-colored hammocks without the strings. Even though they could not be hung, they would make good ground coverings. They were also issued mosquito nets, one for each couple.

But the *piece de resistance* were the uniforms. Regular prison-type garb with faded maroon and gray stripes. They had been especially constructed to fit Americans and really fit very well, but they just were not made for women. Betty told the men there was no way she could fit in hers, and they did not make an issue of her wearing it. But the others dutifully donned their degrading prison apparel.

Later the camp commander, promptly dubbed "Glorious Leader," came by and noticed how ridiculous Carolyn and Lil looked. He merely said, "Hummmph!" If orders had been given for them to wear the ridiculous outfits, he would not cause any officer to lose face by rescinding previously given instructions, even if he disapproved.

At dinner time they were again given all the rice they could eat. More in fact, and they sent much of it back to the camp cook. They were amazed at the quantities of rice the South Vietnamese army officers billeted near them could consume.

"Rice has so little nutritional value that they must eat lots of it to maintain health," Lil explained. As the only foreigner with medical training she felt a responsibility to protect everyone's health. "We really should force ourselves to eat more. Maybe we can get used to it."

"I'm already used to it," Paul grumbled. "How about a steak?"

As darkness crept into the camp they put down split bamboo pads, then tried to lay out the tarps in their "house." It was a close fit. Each person had about two feet by six in which to lie down. Besides a total lack of privacy, it was impossible to even turn over without disturbing neighbors.

This was particularly hard for Betty. The five-foot-ten, big-boned woman needed every inch of space she was allotted. "Help me not to complain," she prayed, remembering the message from Philippians 2:14. "If only You will get word to my children, I'll make it all right, Lord. Please comfort them. Give them assurance I'm all right."

The next morning one of the junior officers came to inform them they could go to the river and bathe. After more than a week a dip in the river seemed a special treat indeed.

"And while you are there, you are to wash those uniforms and return them to us clean. Then you will wear your own clothes," he told the women.

Apparently the Glorious Leader had decided he could now cancel the orders comfortably.

Paul pulled his one and only bar of soap from his bag, "We'll have to make this last just as long as we can," he warned.

They hurried to the river, the women going upstream a short distance where they would have more privacy. The guards didn't seem worried about their taking off into the jungle. The women jumped and played and cavorted in the refreshing stream like carefree schoolgirls. It felt good to be clean, even if they had to be miserly with the soap.

Feeling exhilarated, they returned to the stockade to soak up some sunshine. "If only I could talk to my children for just a few minutes and tell them I'm all right, that we aren't being mistreated," Betty sighed.

"Oh, yes," Lil agreed. "And I think of my parents, too. They're in their eighties and I can't help but wonder if, well, if the shock of our captivity has been too hard on them. Surely they must have heard by now."

"At least you know your families are safe," Carolyn reminded. "I'd be happy right now just to know where my other children are," she said softly as she sat combing LuAnne's flaxen hair.

"They're in school, Mommy," she said. "Don't you remember? We left them there."

"Yes, Sweetie," Carolyn replied gently. "But Uncle Jim Cooper might decide that it would be best for the school to move to Saigon because of the fighting. We know the Coopers will take good care of them, don't we?"

LuAnne nodded contentedly, then ran to watch Ike who was fashioning spoons out of bamboo.

"I'm sorry," Lil murmured. "We shouldn't complain. We do know our children are safe."

"I understand," Carolyn murmured disconsolately.

"I just remembered something," Betty interjected. "Today is March 17. It's Pat Johnson's fifteenth birthday. And we don't even know if her parents are alive."

A somber hush fell on the missionaries as they thought of the thin, dark-haired young teen who enjoyed such a close relationship with her parents.

"I think she really made a good adjustment to living in Vietnam, you know," Lil commented. "Coming to a mission field at eleven is much different from being born here. But she made friends right away and jumped right into athletics and such."

"She always struck me as rather serious," Carolyn added. "Very open and honest, but at the same time quite self-disciplined and conscientious. Serious-minded."

"Yes, in a way she is," Betty remarked, "but she loved to tease her dad. I've seen them go round and round together. It was a real joy to see how much they loved each other, and it made me realize how much my girls have missed out on since Archie has been gone.

"It does make me sad, though, to think that she read *No Time for Tombstones* during Christmas vacation. Under the circumstances, I think it would have been better if she hadn't read the book."

"My kids read it, too," Carolyn added.

"So did ours," said Lil.

"What's that?" Paul asked.

"It's a book about an Alliance nurse, Betty Olsen, and a Wycliffe translator, Hank Blood, who were captured from Banmethuot in 1968," Betty explained.

"Oh?" Peter interposed, all curious. "What happened to them?"

"They died on the trail," the women said in unison.

"Not exactly encouraging," the Australian mused.

They had reason to become even more discouraged that afternoon when guards came and confiscated their belongings. Manuscripts. Reading material. Money. Watches. Jewelry. Everything except their clothes. Pulling off her wedding ring, Betty felt the tug all the way to her heart. But she didn't complain.

"All will be returned," Happy assured them with his false smile. "We are taking them merely for safekeeping. You will get them back." His words seemed hollow and brought no comfort.

That night they downed their tasteless rice and grease soup despondently. They had received no word about the fate of Joan and Norm Johnson. They didn't know if their manuscripts and other belongings would ever be returned. Nor did they have any inkling of how long they would be kept at Camp Sunshine, or even if they would see their loved ones again.

After the meal, Carolyn and Lil excused themselves. More than answering nature's call, it was a chance to talk in privacy.

They swapped stories about their children and even managed to laugh a little. Then Lil's mood suddenly darkened.

Grit, Grime and Grace / 59

"Don't worry," Carolyn assured. "The Lord is looking after the kids."

"I know that," Lil replied listlessly, "but when I think of the manuscripts taken from us. All that work, with Dick making himself sick—for nothing. And when I think of all the time you and John have put in, the dangers you exposed your children to, all to get the Word into the Bru language . . ."

Carolyn smiled at her friend, "I'd feel as bad as you do, except for what a Bru lay pastor once told me. It was at a time when we felt a real sense of urgency. We didn't know how much longer we had in Vietnam and we were assigned to the children's home. We were having difficulty getting language helpers to come to Nhatrang so we could keep up the translation work.

"Just when I felt under the most pressure, this pastor said, 'There are many ways God could have chosen to get His Word to us Bru people. He could have sent it down from heaven. He didn't do that. He could have sent a Bru out to study and learn other languages. He didn't do that. He chose you and your husband to come and learn our language. So I reason, if this is His time and He wants us to have His Word, then He'll see to it we get it.'

"That lifted a big burden from me, Lil. Because, naturally, he was right. We aren't responsible for results. We're only responsible to do what He gives us the strength and wisdom and opportunity and helpers to do. He will see to the results. So I figure if nothing more ever comes of our work, it still has been worth it. We've seen the impact on the Bru tribe of portions of Scripture already translated. It has been well worth it. Even if we should die here, it has been worth it all.

"But I haven't given up hope. They promised to return our stuff. Perhaps they just wanted to inspect everything."

Lil had been listening thoughtfully. She knew Carolyn was right and, with conviction, said, "We'll just keep on praying.

God knows what He's doing."

The gong woke everyone at 5:30 the next morning. They took turns going to the river, then cleaned up around their living quarters and had breakfast.

"I spotted a couple of butterflies down by the river," Lil said. "I wish I could catch some for my kids. They had a really nice collection that we had to leave in Banmethuot. I'd love to get some replacements for them."

"I have a piece of netting the guards didn't take," Paul offered. "Maybe you can make a butterfly net. It'll be interesting to see how many you can find around here."

Lil busied herself fashioning the makeshift net. Ike was proving to be quite proficient with his long knife and was making serviceable spoons. Dick decided to create some games to help pass the time. He started with "Sorry." Because of his fluency in Vietnamese, Jay spent much of his time talking with the other prisoners. Peter and Paul amused themselves with whispered plans of escape they knew were impossible. Carolyn spent a good deal of her time keeping LuAnne occupied. John worked on making more and better bamboo chopsticks.

And Betty thought about Archie.

Had he spent the time they had been separated in a place like this, just sitting around? She doubted that, for the Viet Cong who took him had said they needed medical aid. It seemed reasonable that Archie and Dan Gerber would have been put to work assisting Dr. Vietti. Surely the Communists wouldn't have kept him all this time unless they found him useful.

Perhaps they might all wind up in the same prison camp. She knew the Lord's timing was always perfect, even if Peter, Paul, and Jay cursed the fate that had brought them to Banmethuot just in time for the attack. She felt confident that the Lord had allowed her to be captured for some specific purpose. She prayed that purpose might include reunion with her husband, but whatever it was she knew that all things would work together for good to those who love God. That thought gave her a peace that transcended all the wearisome circumstances.

The women and LuAnne went for their bath that afternoon, leisurely taking their time, for this had become the highlight of their day. About four o'clock they decided they had spent as much time at the river as they could get away with and began the climb back up the hill to their hut.

About halfway up they saw one of the *bo doi* coming, leading a couple of new prisoners. The Johnsons! A dirtier, grimier, more unkempt pair they had never seen, but Norm and Joan looked beautiful. They all fell into each other's arms.

"Oh, I thought you were gone!" Joan sobbed, her tears making muddy tracks down her dusty cheeks. "We saw the men sitting up there in a hut and I thought they had separated the men and women and I'd either be taken from Norm or I'd still be the only woman with all the male prisoners. I'm so glad to see you, but I'm such a mess. I've never felt so filthy in all my life. I've had no change of clothes, no bath, no nothing for over a week."

And indeed they both looked crusty. They had just endured a seven-hour ride on the hot, dusty trail from the Rose Garden.

"I feel so wretched," Joan moaned to her friends.

"Don't worry," Betty consoled. "We'll find you some clean clothes. You go on down to the river and bathe and we'll bring them to you."

"And I have a comb and you can use the soap," Carolyn confided. "We'll get you all fixed up."

When the Johnsons rejoined the group at the hut later Joan sighed, "I feel human again." She was wearing Lil's blouse, Carolyn's slacks, and borrowed underclothes, but she was clean and neat at last.

"Well, tell us where you have been. What happened since we saw you last?" John asked.

"It's been a hard week," Norm confessed, shaking his head, "a hard, hard week."

Road leading into the Raday village below the Alliance compound at Banmethuot. It was along this road that Betty Olsen, Hank Blood, and Mike Benge were led away as captives in 1968. Seven years later Joan and Norman Johnson were seized and taken away along this same road.

4

A Hard Week

Now that Norm and Joan felt human again, they were eager to tell their story. And their colleagues in captivity were even more eager to hear it.

"I think we all knew Sunday night at church that time was running out fast," Norm recalled. "After leaving you we went home and fixed a makeshift bunker in the concrete shower stall that had been added onto our wood house. It seemed the safest place. I put the ironing board across the top to stop some of the debris in case the tin roof should come down. Then I threw a blanket in there and a coat and some medical supplies.

"While I was doing that Joan packed a suitcase and tote bag. Then we went to bed. I guess we should have accepted Betty's invitation to stay with her, but we felt secure in our home and went right to sleep.

"And then all the noise started about three. Boy, that was really something! We were used to rockets during our two years in Danang, but nothing like that. There they'd send in rockets nearly every Sunday at 2:00 A.M. for fifteen or twenty minutes. But it was like rain in Banmethuot. Just continual showers of artillery, rockets, mortars, you know."

They all knew.

"Well, we curled up in our shower stall—it's only about four by four. We didn't fit too well, but we laid in there someway. We knew they were aiming for the Twenty-third Division beyond the compound, but they sure were missing it. We could feel the house shaking and there was a lot of debris, rocks, and stuff coming down on our house.

"We sure were worried about you. It was tough hearing so many explosions coming from the direction of the compound and not knowing if you had been hit or not. All we could do was pray for you.

"It was really scary. But we just stayed all squinched up in there and spent three and a half hours just praying and singing hymns and quoting Scripture. We prayed for the Vietnamese, the Raday, the Christians back home in Canada, and especially for our kids. Not just Pat and Doug, but all our kids.

"Suddenly it got quiet. We didn't know what was going on, but we hoped it was over. We waited for the sound of small arms fire. As long as the big stuff was coming in we knew no troops would be coming, but then we heard the small arms start.

"About 6:30, I left Joan in the shower stall and ran to the front bedroom window and looked out. I saw some Raday people standing across the street so I went out to talk to them. They crossed over toward me and we just stood there in the middle of the street talking. It really sounds stupid now, because there were explosions all around us. Small explosions and bullets zinging by. It was really weird, us standing there asking each other what to do. You know, 'Are you going to the jungle?' 'Are you going to try to get into the city?' 'What shall we do?' Then I said, 'I think my wife and I will go up to the compound.'

"Suddenly we heard this great big yell like a football team coming on the field. The NVA had crossed that bridge at the bottom of our street. It was three or four blocks away, but we could hear them cheering.

"Well, by this time Joan had come to the front door and saw me standing there like a dummy talking to the Raday. She called, 'Get off the street! What are you doing out there?' That was the same time we heard the yell from the NVA, and we all scattered. The Raday ran back to their houses, and I had started up the street when there was an explosion right in front of me. In the air, so close I could have touched it. I was just looking right into this ball of fire and smoke.

"But I didn't hear anything—maybe I got a concussion, but I wasn't even scratched. It was really fantastic that my eardrums weren't blasted. All I know is that there was a flash, and then I was crawling up the ditch that ran along the side of the road."

"A Raday woman was injured," Joan interrupted. "I saw her holding her forehead; she was bleeding from a shrapnel wound. A man ran over to help her. I just picked up our things and ran out there."

"Yeah, she had the blanket and jacket and the valise and tote bag, and I was carrying nothing," Norm continued. "Everything happened so fast and was so confusing, you know. So we went to the Raday house beside us because they had a bunker there.

"It was full of Vietnamese. And then some more came and they were standing outside. So I said, 'Honey, we can't stay here. This isn't our bunker. Come on, we'll have to get out of here.'

"So we left and they went in the bunker. And we just stood there. Waiting. We didn't know what to do. Then I said, 'Let's try the house behind us.' So we ran over and climbed the barbed wire fence. And Joan's pant leg got caught. There we were, trying to free her and the NVA coming up the street."

"Oh, it was so scary," Joan interjected. "All the shooting and the explosions."

"Well, I got her loose and we made it to the other bunker. Our neighbors were in there, huddled together, and they let us come in. These were tribespeople. An older lady, a child, and a teenager, and then Joan and I. Five of us in a bunker that was maybe four by five. It was just a hole in the ground at the back of their house with a wooden platform pulled over the top.

"We could see through the slats in the platform and debris was falling in on us, so we held the blanket over our heads. It was junky down there, but we felt a lot safer. We stayed there from about 7:45 in the morning until 4:00 in the afternoon. And during all that time we could hear the NVA walking all around. Talking. Shooting. Lots of shooting. And explosions. We could hear them ordering people out of their houses and hiding places. They were taking them out of the village.

"Finally, they got to our house. We heard a loud explosion. Whether they threw something in there I don't know. But we could hear them in our kitchen, knocking pots and pans around. Then they must have gone into my study, 'cause I heard someone yell, 'Canadians live here. Here's a Canadian flag!'

"Then they went out in the street and yelled to the villagers. 'Where are the Canadians?' Somebody yelled back—it sounded like a tribesperson—'I don't know. They went out.' They were speaking Vietnamese, but it sounded like a tribesman saying, 'Maybe they went up to the highway or into the city.'

"So about that time they spotted our car and one said, 'Let's go for a joy ride.' But they were just talking and went back into the house.

"The strange thing is that all this time there was plenty of shooting, plenty of explosions, and the planes were bombing—and these guys were calmly going about doing their duty. They were absolutely courageous and so well disciplined. The planes were bombing heavily and the debris was falling down on us in the bunker—and they were out there walking around. Then someone started playing our piano! Can you believe that? With all that shooting and exploding and bombing, he was playing our piano!

"And we were down there praying. When the bombing was heavy and there was lots of noise we'd sing, and in between we would just pray in our hearts. But we were plenty scared, I tell you!

"About four o'clock they found us. They shot into the ground a few times and said, 'Come on, get out of there.' So we climbed out, and they were surprised to see foreigners. They must have thought we had gone into the city. The first thing they asked us was, 'Where is the radio?' We didn't have a radio; we didn't know what they were talking about."

"I had a radio," Paul explained. "We had been talking to a plane from the USAID compound. They must have been listening in."

"Oh. Well, they seemed to think we had been giving locations from the bunker. Directing planes. Which was ridiculous. We couldn't see anything from down in there. So they marched us off to the corner. We left all our stuff in the bunker."

"Yes, and we had two hundred dollars in our valise that belonged to a Raday church," Joan added. "We really felt bad about leaving that. We know how hard it was for them to save all that money. They'd given it to us to buy them a pump organ."

"Well, they got us down to this little command post down at the corner, in a bunker right across the street from where Vange and Hank Blood used to live. One soldier started to tie me up and the officer came out and pulled his revolver from his holster. And there was no reason for that unless he meant to use it, 'cause the others already had guns on me. I really thought when he pulled the gun he was going to kill me right there.

"But I said, 'Don't be afraid of me'—which seems like a dumb thing to say under the circumstances, but the words just seemed to tumble out of my mouth. I said, 'Don't be afraid of me. If you tell me to sit down, I'll sit down. If you tell me to go over there, I'll go over there. Please don't be afraid of me. I'm a missionary. Don't tie me up.'

"Whatever he had in his mind, he said to the soldier, 'Untie this man.' And they had really tied me hard, behind the back by the biceps. Really tight. So he said, 'Untie this man, and give him his watch and his money back.'

"Then after talking a little bit they led us out of the village into the hills to the south. We walked across the same bridge they had come in on, then across the fields to the higher area. And while we were crossing those fields planes were strafing and rocketing. I was really worried, 'cause here we were with the enemy troops crossing fields with the planes so low you could almost touch the dumb things. They were dive bombing and we could see the rockets leaving the planes. Shooting at tanks moving through our area. I was really scared we might get strafed.

"The NVA said, 'Don't worry.' But he was watching the planes himself.

"So we were marching out as the enemy soldiers were marching in. There was a teenaged Vietnamese boy with us. Don't know where they got him. Whoever he was he stayed with us as we sat on a hillside until about eight that night. We could see the Raday church still standing. Then soldiers came and marched us off with some South Vietnamese prisoners and a wounded woman. I don't know how she got with us. There was a lot of confusion.

"We started walking. I tried to figure where we were by the stars. We were going parallel with Highway 14, heading straight for the Cambodian border. Then we swung north, and all I could think of was Danang. Then we turned again, east I think. I kept remembering that map in *No Time for Tombstones,* and I believe we went the same way those captives were taken.

"We walked very slowly; there were a number of injured with us. And it was a really rough trail, through rivers and up hills. Joan broke her sandles along the way.

"We wound up making a circle and coming right back to Banmethuot. On our side of the village, but farther away. It was one o'clock by the time we got back. That was a long, hard walk for nothing. I don't know why they did that. Maybe just to get us disoriented. I don't know.

"Then we sat on the hillside and watched the rockets going into the city. And the huge fires burning."

"Fires?" the others wanted to know.

"Oh, yeah, there were huge fires. We thought it was the heart of the city burning. Later we found out it was fuel dumps and stuff. Fantastic fires! We asked what was burning and they told us the whole city was on fire. And we didn't know where you guys were.

"Then they took the civilian woman away, and Joan had lent her her sweater, so that was the end of that. A large group of soldiers came and said, 'Come with us.' We got in front of them and marched off into the darkness. I thought we were going to be executed for sure. I just figured they were taking the whole batch of us off to kill us.

"Well, they took us and put us in a cement building and locked the door. We were under guard, Joan and I, along with some South Vietnamese soldiers and tribespeople. We looked around in this big room and saw bodies, lots of them, covered by tarps and blankets. Really gruesome. They told us to lie down so we did, but we didn't know what was going on.

"Later on, some of the 'bodies' moved and made noises and we knew they were alive. But that was the strangest feeling when we thought we were lying there with dead people. Finally we fell asleep, but at five in the morning, well, somewhere about then—it was still dark—the South Vietnamese planes came and *they* bombed us.

"This was early Tuesday morning and we were really frightened, because the bombs were falling quite near. The tension was really strong in there. It wasn't the least bit comforting to know those were South Vietnamese planes.

"When it got light and there was no more bombing the NVA took us out and lined us up on the two sides of this long road. There were some civilians in the group, oriental-looking Vietnamese and round-eyed tribesmen. All men. Joan was the only woman."

"Which was scary for me," Joan admitted. "But I remembered in *Tombstones* that Betty Olsen was never molested, and that helped. No one ever made any advances."

"Well, sometime that morning they gave us some rice," Norm continued, "and some kind of sweet potato stuff. But nobody cared to eat. We weren't even hungry and we hadn't eaten since Sunday evening. They gave us some water from the river. Unboiled. We were so thirsty we drank it anyway.

"While we were sitting on the side of the road the NVA started getting information from all the prisoners. Making out reports on each of us. They kept asking us how many foreigners were in Banmethuot and we said, 'Five and a child,' 'cause we were just thinking of the missionaries. Sorry, guys," he apologized, looking at Paul, Peter, Ike, and Jay.

"So night came again and they put us in another building. A big room with about a hundred in there. About four o'clock the airplanes came back and started bombing again. I mean right up to the front doorstep. Clusters of explosions. Big ones. Large explosions. It was really frightening. Everyone would sit up and stand in groups. The South Vietnamese soldiers were all tied together. They were scared, too.

"The next morning—let's see, that would be Wednesday morning—they took us back outside, and we've been outside ever since. We just slept on the roadside or under coffee plants.

"And we recognized some Christians!" he exclaimed, getting all excited. "Y Ta was there! He's the pastor of the Raday church," Norm explained to the four nonmissionaries. "But he never spoke to us, and we didn't let on that we knew him. We didn't want to get him in trouble. Boy, would we have loved to talk with him, 'cause we had no idea of what was going on. We didn't know if you'd been captured or what.

"We just saw him by the side of the road, and he cried and cried. Guess he was thinking about us and the situation. But we never got to talk with him.

"We talked with some of the Vietnamese, but we were suspicious. We didn't know but that they were spies. So we were very careful and didn't talk much.

"We did talk some to Y Ting. He came and told us he had tried to deliver your message that you were going to the city, but he had been captured at the top of our street and never got to tell us. So we knew you were trying to get to the USAID compound, but didn't know if you made it. We couldn't get out of the village anyway, so we were glad you went without us. At least we knew everybody had survived the night and you were all right when he left you.

"We didn't want the NVA to know we knew Y Ting, so we looked off in the other direction and just spoke a few words at a time so the guards couldn't tell we were talking to him. There was another Raday Christian we knew. I sat looking at Joan and talking to him in Raday, and he was pretending to talk to another Raday. But he didn't know much.

"Of course, by this time Joan and I were in pretty bad shape. Dirty. Messy. We didn't want to get too close to anyone. We just stayed there for nearly a week. Drank out of the jungle stream. Slept in the ditch. No mosquito nets. They used to take us away from the rest of the group to eat our meals. The others were given lectures and I guess they didn't want us to hear.

"Other than that we weren't allowed to move around at all. All we did was sit. Just sit. We kept asking the guards for water, and they'd give us some from their canteens and that was boiled. But it was hot and we'd get so thirsty we'd lap it up from the river. With our hands, you know. We really bugged them about not having boiled water. They got better about that.

"We did get plenty of rice, and once a tin of meat, Spamlike. Twice we had half a lime apiece. Mostly just rice and fish powder. That was rank. Just awful, but we needed the protein.

"Then they separated us from the others. Put us off in the plantation near a couple of Vietnamese Catholic priests who had been captured in their cossacks. They were just a few feet from us, but not close enough to talk to.

"We sure wondered what happened to the rest of you. The NVA kept asking us how many foreigners were in Banmethuot. We'd tell them, and then we'd ask what happened to you.

"We were very close to the old leprosarium. We could see the radio tower, so we knew the general direction of where we were. And we knew Archie and the others had been taken near there," Norm told Betty, "so we inquired about them. But they didn't seem to know anything. I think they were telling the truth.

"We asked why we were being kept. We weren't soldiers. We weren't military personnel. We were just missionaries. And we wanted to go home and be with our children and our families. The political officer told us, 'You people are not pris-

A Hard Week / 73

oners of war, we are just keeping you here for your own protection.' "

"Oh, yeah, sure!" came the disbelieving cries of the others.

"Well, there's some truth in that," Norm conceded, "because one day a soldier came up to us—that was after they had taken us to the end of the road away from the other prisoners. Anyway, this soldier came and said, 'I'm going to shoot you dead tonight.' Boy, I tell you, we really thought this is it. So we just prayed that the Lord would protect us, that we were committed to Him. If it was His will to take us, we were ready. So we just trusted the Lord.

"We sang hymns again; that really helped. But another soldier heard us and came over and said, 'You can't sing.' Before we had been told, 'Don't sing so loud.' I guess they didn't want the other prisoners to hear us singing. But this time when he said not to sing at all, we just couldn't understand it.

"So then the political officer came up and asked, 'What's wrong?' And I said to him, 'If you are going to kill us, why not kill us now? Why wait until tonight?' He said, 'Who told you that?' And I told him about the soldier telling us he was going to shoot us dead that night, and he said, 'Well, we're not going to do anything like that.'

"After he moved us to another spot the foot soldiers never came near us again. The only people who came to us were officers and political cadres. The Lord really protected us.

"There was one nice old man who told us, 'You two don't worry about a thing, you will see your children again. Before very long. I am the chief, and I tell the truth. I do not lie. The Vietnamese never lie.'

"So this really encouraged us. Hearing that from the man who was in charge. He told us, 'I promise you the Liberation Army will never lie, and I say that you will see your children soon.'

"He was really a nice old man. He said, 'You believe in

Jesus Christ, but we believe in Ho Chi Minh. You believe in Christianity, but we believe in materialism.'

"So when they woke us at 2:30 A.M. on March 17, our daughter Pat's birthday, and told us we were going to a better, nicer place, we believed them. Figured we were going to be released. They loaded up three or four, or maybe five, trucks. We drove through Banmethuot about four o'clock, saw a lot of burned-out tanks, and we went to the north of the city, then turned northwest toward Ban Don, to the camp where you had been kept."

"The Rose Garden?" they all exploded. "That was the 'nicer' place? What a joke."

"You named that camp the Rose Garden?" Joan asked incredulously. Then she and Norm realized the irony of it and burst into laughter. "Well, it certainly is a fragrant place," Norm conceded.

"But we liked it because we found out you were alive. We saw some Raday prisoners who knew Betty and they told us how many there were of you, and the little girl. They all remembered LuAnne. They told us all of you were all right and that you had left the day before.

"And they told us Y Ngue, the district superintendent of all the tribal churches, was there, but he was in another section of the camp and we didn't get to talk with him. But I noticed one man there who was not Vietnamese. At first I couldn't figure who he was, but later found out he was an Iranian ICCS* man. Also the Indonesian ICCS member was there. They had been captured and brought to this camp.

"I ran over to them before any of the soldiers could stop me, 'cause I knew they wouldn't keep a member of the International Control Commission for long. I told them, 'Please, do you remember me? I'm a Canadian. If you don't remember my name, just remember I'm a Canadian. If you get out, tell somebody that we're alive and try to get word to our children in

*International Commission of Control and Supervision

Penang, Malaysia, so they'll know we are not dead.' And I told them to say that all the missionaries—all the foreigners got out of Banmethuot alive."

"Praise the Lord!" Betty exclaimed.

"We've all been praying that some word could get out to reassure our families," Lil added.

"If anybody is released, it'll be ICCS guys," Paul commented. "And a story about our safety will surely be picked up by the wire services around the world. I'm sure our families will hear it."

Here was the second miraculous answer to prayer in one day. First the Johnsons were with them, and now word had been sent to their loved ones.

"At least we're together now," Joan signed. "It's such a relief to be with you."

With two more "guests," the foreigners' hut was more crowded than ever that night. They had to sleep right up against each other, but no one minded.

5

Life in "Camp Sunshine"

The prisoners wriggled from their cramped positions and stretched to remove the kinks of another cool night spent sleeping on the ground. In a couple of hours they would be sweltering in the jungle heat.

Norm looked at his ragged, tattered clothes. "I'm going to ask our friend Happy for a new outfit."

When Happy was not accommodating, John rummaged in the pile of gear brought along from the Land Rover. "Try these on," he suggested, handing Norm a pair of wrinkled walking shorts.

The women turned while Norm changed.

"Well, I'm ready to leave now," he announced. "They have us all together so they might as well just release us en masse."

"Dreamer," scoffed the Aussie, Peter.

"It would help if we only knew how long," Joan commented.

Betty didn't look so grim. "I know every possible pressure is being put on the North Vietnamese."

"How do you know that?" Jay demanded.

"Because I know how our officials in the Alliance have worked to get Archie and the two other missionaries captured with him released. I'm sure they're doing as much for us."

"Just what have they done for your husband?" Paul inquired eagerly. "What channels have they worked through?"

"Dr. Louis King—he's our foreign secretary, uh, director—first approached the American National Red Cross. They got in touch with the International Committee of the Red Cross in Geneva. Dr. Nathan Bailey, our president, tried to work through the Cambodian Red Cross. The Canadian government and the British Foreign Office also made some contacts. And, of course, the U.S. State Department, the Department of Defense, and the CIA all tried to find him. Plus different religious organizations such as the Mennonite Central Committee and the National Council of Churches. And a number of U.S. senators. Even Prince Sihanouk tried to find out their whereabouts, but the National Liberation Front always denied any knowledge of their capture.

"Our people will keep trying," Betty added hopefully.

Paul was impressed. "With all that pressure, surely you missionaries will be released."

"What about us?" Ike asked uneasily. His eyes were on Paul.

"The missionaries were involved in strictly humanitarian work. As we have been also. But the NVA may be a little more suspicious of us because we're employed by the State Department. And without a doubt they'll question the appearance of Peter and Jay just before the beginning of their big offensive. Can't blame them for doing so. Still, maybe we all have a chance, if there's a lot of concern. Particularly if the U.N. should go to bat for us."

"Don't forget the people who are praying," Lil reminded.

"Our families and churches. Why, my whole home church is probably praying around the clock."

"Yes, and there are thousands of Christians around the world praying who have only heard of us," Betty put in. "When I was last home on furlough, everywhere I went people would come up and say they were praying for Archie, Dan, and Ardel. They'll be praying for us, too."

"And our Wycliffe folks," John interspersed. "We have a worldwide network sending out prayer alert bulletins. I guarantee we're on that net."

"We're enveloped by prayer," Joan assured. "I really don't think we'd all be alive and well otherwise."

The other missionaries were agreeing. The comfort showed on their faces. Paul, Ike, Peter, and Jay just smiled a little and shrugged skeptically.

"Let's really ask the Lord that the ICCS men get the word out that we are all safe here," Betty proposed. "I know the torture of not knowing if your loved one is okay. I don't want my kids going through that." For an instant Betty's self-control broke as tears welled up in her eyes.

"Uh, I need to go for a walk," Joan mentioned in obvious understanding. "Want to come with me?"

Betty smiled valiantly and the two left.

"What kind of person is Archie?" Peter asked when the two were out of earshot.

"Kind," Lil replied quickly. "A big, strong man, but very gentle. And gregarious. Always wore a smile. He and Betty made a perfect pair.

"I remember one time before Dick and I married and I was nursing at the clinic in Dalat. A Koho tribesboy died. He was a long way from home. I went to the school there where Archie and Betty were houseparents and told him my dilemma. He was so understanding. 'Don't worry,' he said. 'I'll take care of everything.'

"He made a coffin, or had some of his tribal workers help

him. I'm not sure which. But he could make or fix anything. Well, he brought the coffin over to the clinic in his Land Rover. Then we drove the body out to the cemetery where the boy's relatives who worked at the Dalat School came for a beautiful burial service. Archie had gotten in touch with them.

"That incident stands out in my memory because it was so very like Archie. He could take over in any situation. Very dependable. And caring. He really cared for people."

"I only met him once," John recalled. "I had stopped by the Alliance school for some reason or other and spent the night. We played a game of tennis. He was pretty good. A big, affable man. The type you like right away. He and Betty really seemed to be excellent houseparents."

"Oh, they were," Lil interrupted. "They were so good with those kids. Made them feel like one big family. They'd take them on picnics and hikes and trips and plan special things on Friday nights. Betty would make taffy or they'd pop popcorn and play games—to make an event of it."

"I can remember when I used to think just anybody could be houseparents," Carolyn commented. "Then we were given the job for a year with our Wycliffe kids. Now I don't think anyone can do it. It's really a task."

"Yes," Lil agreed. "But they did it with a lot of love and dedication. And they tried very hard not to be partial toward their own children and still make them feel special. That's really tough."

When Betty and Joan returned Lil and Carolyn excused themselves. They preferred the bushes by the river to the open holes used by the men. Also, they had the opportunity to talk in more privacy.

They talked about their children and their work. They prayed together for a moment or two, asking God to keep their kids strong, and for the return of the manuscripts, if this was His will.

Life in "Camp Sunshine" / 81

That very afternoon the guards lugged in their belongings which had been classified as having no military value. The first thing the missionaries looked for were the precious manuscripts that represented so many years of toil. They were there. Intact. Another answer to prayer!

The Millers' paraphernalia when spread out looked like a display in a second-hand store. "The Lord knew what we needed," Norm said almost jubilantly. Much of the equipment was very practical: tools, such as pliers and screwdriver; glue and epoxy; measuring cups, six glasses with straws, dishes, and Tupperware; typewriter; and sewing machine with needles and thread in a drawer.

Tennis rackets and balls were pounced on. Playing word games couldn't take the place of physical exercise. Besides, Dick had already established himself as champion of that pastime.

Best of all, their Bibles. "Thank you, Lord, oh, thank you," Betty rejoiced, clutching her Bible tightly.

The potpourri of possessions helped the days pass more rapidly and profitably. The translators worked on their manuscripts. The women sewed. Joan mended the rip in her blue slacks. Lil made a yarn doll for LuAnne. Everyone enjoyed playing catch.

LuAnne, who had remained amazingly healthy, continued to charm everyone. The guards were captivated by her shy, pixie smile and did little favors for her. Even Happy grinned when she opened her morning glory eyes at him. In appreciation he bequeathed a small ointment tin for play.

She often enjoyed looking at photos of her brothers and sister. "Here is Nathan," she would say. "And Gordon. Oh, see Margie."

Snapshots were a source of encouragement to the others as they passed around pictures of their loved ones. Betty loved to explain to the Vietnamese prisoners, "You call me 'Grandmother.' Well, I really am one," and she would hold up a colored photo of Rachel at three months.

One night John delighted LuAnne by pulling out his harmonica and playing for her as she drifted off to sleep. Then the others started singing along. It was the first of many evenings' entertainment.

The missionaries were a bit surprised to learn that Peter had a remarkable repertoire of hymns. His mellow baritone added a touch of real class to the harmony.

His favorite was "How Great Thou Art." The Australian confided that he had once attended a Billy Graham crusade, although he didn't sound too impressed. "I was raised as an altar boy in the Church of England," he explained. "I had enough religion instilled in me to last for the rest of my life."

The time of singing and sharing the promises of God kept up the spirits of the missionaries. The others appeared to enjoy the singing, too, but were noncommittal about spiritual convictions. It was for all a pleasant way to spend the dark hours of the evening and they awoke with more contentment the morning after.

One morning when Betty was writing in her pocket-sized black diary, Happy came by and noticed. To everyone's surprise he chirped, "Good. Very good. You should all keep diaries of your stay. It will give you something worthwhile to do and will be a good souvenir to take home."

Even though there were now nearly a thousand prisoners in the camp tension had lessened. At night, along with the hymn singing, the foreigners harmonized on secular tunes which expressed their desires, such as, "Don't Fence Me In," "Leaving on a Jet Plane," and "Release Me."

Paul even walked around singing with a Nashville twang, "I've got tears in my ears, from lying on my back crying over you."

"Oh, Paul," Carolyn laughed, "you just made that up."

"Nope, it's a song. Good old country and western." And he sang another verse. She came back with, "I'm Leaving on a Jet Plane."

Then the atmosphere changed. First it was an order for some of the black-uniformed Vietnamese and tribal POWs to begin digging in a place marked off about four feet wide and forty feet long. All the foreigners were apprehensive about what such a large trench would be used for, but didn't feel free to ask questions.

Then it was conflict over getting permission to go to the river. The rules specified that a prisoner was to ask a guard for permission by giving his/her name, where he/she wanted to go, and why. Upon returning, this information was to be repeated and permission requested to reenter the stockade.

The whole procedure seemed quite unnecessary, and for the women humiliating. They had become a little lax. Sometimes they would ask permission of one guard to leave and obtain another *bo doi's* approval to reenter. This confused the guards who were intent on following every letter of the law. When the officer who had previously decided they didn't have to wear the uniforms learned about the problem, he exploded.

"You do not have the proper attitude!" he yelled, with Jay interpreting. "You are being uncooperative! You will obey all rules of this camp! From this time you will ask me, personally, for permission to go to the river. I am in charge. You will speak to me when you need to go and when you must return. Do you understand?"

They all nodded gravely, and from that time on this officer was called "Bathman."

It appeared to the foreigners that the national prisoners had been warned not to have much to do with them, but with so many corralled in such a small area, some communication was inevitable. Because Jay spoke Vietnamese fluently and enjoyed good rapport with the nationals, he often drifted from hut to hut, talking with black-uniformed prisoners for hours at a time.

The Raday captives frequently came to talk with Betty. Because of her years spent working in the leprosy clinic and visiting tribal villages on evangelistic trips she knew many of the tribespeople. If she didn't know someone personally, she usually could recall a friend they had in common. She showed them pictures of Rachel, and they would smile and talk about their children.

After getting to know a group of Raday, Betty would slip them gospel tracts and tell them about Jesus. She encouraged Christian Raday to witness to their fellow prisoners.

"Some good must come from our time in captivity," she would say. "We must be beacons for the Lord among the princes of darkness."

"Yes, yes, Grandmother," the Christians would reply, "we must."

The tribespeople wanted to show Betty appreciation for her friendship. One morning a group brought a basket of tree leaves. Pronouncing them edible, they showed her how to make leaf soup.

The missionaries held their first informal worship service the Sunday before Easter. The four foreign men joined them in singing, and as the music carried across the camp, Vietnamese and tribal POWs began gathering.

Norm Johnson gave a sermon on the resurrection. "Everyone must die at one time or another," he declared, conscious of the many non-Christians in his audience. "Whether Vietnamese, Raday, Australian, American, or whoever, death has always been inevitable. But Jesus, who died on the cross for our sins, could not be conquered by death. On the third day He arose. He lives today and offers eternal life, life after death, to all who will receive Him as their Savior and Lord."

The expressions on the faces of the listeners were very revealing. Some smiled radiantly. Some sat or stood stoically, pondering Norm's message. Others appeared to lean forward, as men starving and thirsting for hope. No one displayed hostility or rancor.

The Communist officers and guards did not observe Sunday and kept the work crew digging the long ditch deeper. The men's latrine was close by the ditch and every time the male foreigners used the facilities, they looked at, and speculated about, the excavation. They kept any opinions they had about the future use to themselves, not wanting to upset the women.

The prisoners awoke the next morning to a cloudy sky. It was March 25. The rainy season would begin any day now.

The cooler air did not dispell any desire for bathing. With only one bar of soap among them, they had adeptly developed a ritual for making the soap last.

A bather would first dunk himself to get wet all over. Then after lathering up his hair, he would squeeze out the bubbles for spreading over his body. Next he would transfer the suds onto his dirty clothes, rinse himself clean, and end the process by washing and rinsing out his clothes. The result wasn't a hundred percent satisfactory, but with one shrinking bar of soap it was the best he could do.

That night after they squeezed into sleeping position they sang awhile and John played his harmonica until LuAnne fell asleep. The women talked softly until Peter's rhythmic snoring lulled everyone to slumber. After a while Peter was disturbed by LuAnne's bony knee pushing against his face. But he was adjusting to her restlessness and managed to turn without becoming wide awake or rousing anyone else.

About 3:00 A.M. the rain began. A cold, steady, soaking rain. There was no hope of keeping dry under the sieve of a roof,

86 / Prisoners of Hope

and the wind was blowing water on them anyway. They sat up and huddled together under the center of the roof, striving to cover themselves with tarps and mosquito nets.

It was useless. Soon they were drenched and sat like drowning rats awaiting the dawn.

Suddenly there was the sound of footsteps, then the beam of a flashlight shining in their eyes. It was only a patrol guard. They heard him murmur something—sympathetically, it seemed to them—then walk on.

But the pity was unnecessary for the Lord gave Carolyn a song of comfort. The lines of "He Giveth More Grace" kept running through her mind the rest of that miserable night.

When we have exhausted our store of endurance,
When our strength has failed ere the day is half done,
When we reach the end of our hoarded resources,
Our Father's full giving is only begun.

His love has no limit; His grace has no measure;
His pow'r has no boundary known unto men
For out of His infinite riches in Jesus,
He giveth, and giveth, and giveth again!

Morning came at last and the bedraggled prisoners draped their bedding on trees and poles around the camp to dry. By the time they were finished the wet ground was already steaming in the warm sun and the POW work crew was digging in the long trench.

The trench was nearly four feet deep now. On their way to the latrine, John and Norm eyed the excavation apprehensively. They hoped it wasn't what they thought.

When Norm returned he was called out for a period of interrogation that lasted most of the day.

"How was it?" his missionary cohorts asked apprehensively

when he finally came back. "What did they ask? Were they rude?"

Norm tried to act blasé. "Oh, mostly the usual stuff. My name, rank, and serial number. How long I had worked for the CIA."

"What did you tell them?" Joan interjected a bit anxiously.

"I gave them the history of our work with the Raday. About teaching in the Bible school. Witnessing. Preaching. I didn't feel I had anything to hide, so I just explained it all.

"The only thing upsetting was what they asked about the other guys," he explained, with a flick of his head toward Peter and Paul who were sitting out of earshot, involved in a deep philosophical discussion. "You know, we really don't know much about them."

"That just might be for the best," Dick commented softly.

After a pregnant pause, John nodded. "Yeah, what we don't know we don't have to worry about revealing. Do you think one of our friends might actually be a spy?"

Dick shrugged.

"Well, we are totally nonpolitical," Carolyn asserted. "And I certainly don't think we should get ourselves involved with anything subversive at this late date."

"Right," Betty concurred, "I don't want to lie. And I don't want to know anything I might have to hide. As it is we have nothing to fear. All we need do is tell the truth."

Lil had been standing in thoughtful silence. "Then we're agreed not to question our four friends too much about their past or their political stands?" she asked.

Except for Norm, their looks showed concurrence. "What's with you?" Joan asked.

"We should also consider the possibility that one of them could be spying for the other side."

"Spying on us?" she gasped.

"Well, thanks, Norm. We really needed that," Carolyn

teased. "It isn't bad enough to be prisoners, now you're going to make us all paranoid, suspecting each other."

All of them chuckled, but none forgot the conversation.

The next day was Peter's twenty-first wedding anniversary, and he was interrogated.

"It wasn't all that bad," the broadcaster reported upon his return. "Actually, they were pretty nice. Gave me a special meal topped off with a cup of coffee."

"Mmmmmmmmmmmmm," the others chorused in envy. "I didn't get any," Norm added, "and I'm better looking than you."

"They were lacking a sense of humor, though," Peter continued. "I gave them the line about having twin sons nineteen and twenty. They weren't the least bit amused when I pointed out they are two sets of twins. Perhaps it lost something in the translation.

"What did stump me was why you missionaries had remained in Banmethuot when the American forces left a couple of years ago. I couldn't explain that even to myself."

"We stayed because we felt needed," Norm retorted, suddenly serious.

"And we felt that was where the Lord wanted us," Carolyn put in determinedly.

"Sorry, but it seems stupid to me," Jay interjected. "Didn't you realize how vulnerable you were there? Do you have some kind of martyr complex?"

"Jay," Betty said kindly, "you can't truly live life to the fullest until you have a faith you're willing to die for."

Jay still didn't comprehend, but, not wanting to argue with the older woman, he shook his head and lapsed into silence.

Betty was becoming more bold in her witnessing and not only talked to fellow prisoners, but shared tracts with the guards as well. They would take her bit of reading material, glance at it, and say, "We don't need this belief now that we

Life in "Camp Sunshine" / 89

have had our revolution." And they would argue. But they'd also keep the tracts.

Arguing with the missionaries got to be rather a sport for the guards. They would never admit any interest and would verbally reject the story of Jesus. One day Lil told a couple of them, "Just remember that you have heard the story of salvation. We did come to Vietnam to tell you of the love of the Lord Jesus. Now the responsibility is yours."

On Good Friday, March 28, they had a time of prayer together after their morning meal. They thanked the Lord especially that they were together. And prayed for strength and wisdom to be good witnesses for Him during the days of their captivity. And, as always, requested a special blessing on their children.

No one mentioned the trench that was now over the heads of the prisoners who were continuing to dig. But later Joan whispered to Norm the question that was plaguing them all, "Is it going to be a mass grave?"

Norm shook his head indecisively and pushed his hands into his pockets. "Don't know. That would be one way of eliminating the population explosion around here." Paul strolled by singing about the "tears in his ears," and they didn't discuss it anymore.

Saturday was much cooler and more humid than any day they had experienced in Camp Sunshine. More thatch had been brought in and a new house was under construction for the foreigners. They hoped it would be leak-proof, but they knew that without walls a windy rain would be drenching.

"Talk about losing weight the hard way," Joan quipped when they began discussing their thinness. "But we really can't blame them. We send rice back after every meal."

"I'll make us something good," Ike proposed. "Keep your extra rice tonight. When I was a boy in the Philippines during World War II, I hid in the hills with the guerillas. I learned many ways to fix rice."

True to his word, the Filipino dumped the extra rice into a large tin can, added water, and began stirring it over the fire. He stirred until the grains dissolved into a porridgelike substance resembling Cream of Rice. Then he ladled the concoction into the others' white plastic bowls and they added milk and sugar from a cache. "Delicious!" was the unanimous decision.

"We call it *chao*," Ike informed them. "We can have three meals a day now by saving the leftovers from the other two."

Thereafter, Ike became the official "foreign" cook.

The next day was Easter Sunday. They began their service by singing gospel hymns. As on the Sunday before, other prisoners heard them and came around the foreigners' shelter to listen in.

John Miller was reading Scripture when Happy spotted the gathering and came over to investigate. "What is this?" the political officer demanded.

"We are just practicing freedom of religion as you gave us permission," John replied.

"We have no objection to your meeting together and singing and reading, but the other prisoners must not come." He then ordered the others away, instructing them not to "bother" the foreigners again during their worship.

After he left they just sang and talked louder so the POWs who wanted to could hear anyway.

That afternoon Paul was called for an interview. When he returned he went through what was becoming a customary debriefing by the rest of the group.

"One of the things that bugged them," the USAID man informed them, "is why I didn't have closer contact with you missionaries when we were all living in Banmethuot. I tried to explain the, uh, difference in our lifestyles."

That got some knowing smiles. The colorful USAID officer's drink and speech habits had given him a lifestyle dramatically different from that of the missionaries.

"I did get one bit of information from them," he continued. "I asked about our status. I said that as civilians we were curious just why we were being detained. Happy informed me that we are now regarded as prisoners of war and that they are keeping us to find out just who we really are. I take it they don't really believe anything we have told them."

News of this classification was depressing. They were further dispirited about 4:30 P.M. when it began to rain, not hard, but enough so that all their things got wet again. When the drizzle stopped an officer came and delivered a political lecture. It sounded just like the others they had heard and no one paid much attention to it. Then their pictures were taken.

LuAnne had developed a case of the sniffles from being exposed to the elements and was complaining about having to go to bed while John was tying up their mosquito net and tucking it under the big blue blanket they used as a ground sheet. He let out a terrible yowl and started dancing around, holding his finger. The rest dashed over to see what had happened. Ike spotted the offender. A scorpion.

Paul dug into his survival bag and produced some Nupercainal ointment which Lil applied to the wound. The anesthetic and some aspirin was all they had to relieve the pain that continued to throb throughout the night. John had already been suffering from stomach cramps and with this added torment he got little sleep.

But the next morning he forgot his discomfort when Norm came galloping back from a trip to the four-seated "throne." "It's a latrine!" he announced joyously. "They're building a bamboo platform over that trench and it's going to be used as a latrine! A big one. Sixteen-eighteen holer." It was quite a relief to be able to laugh at their fears.

Dick was tabbed that day for questioning. He returned earlier than the other men had. When asked what he had told the interrogators he replied, "Not much." The reply was so typical that they all had to laugh at the thought of Dick's living up to his reputation as a man of brevity.

That afternoon they moved into the new house. It was no larger than they had before, but it did have a platform about three feet off the ground, so they no longer had to sleep so near the damp earth. The rainy weather had taken its toll on the prisoners and most had colds. LuAnne's seemed the worst, and both John and Carolyn were now suffering from stomach cramps. The scorpion bite of the night before was still giving John a lot of pain, so as soon as they were moved in he lay down.

To add to John's misery a spider crawled into his ear. The crawling sound and tickling on his eardrum was excruciating. He rolled and twisted in pain. Neither of the nurses knew what to do. Finally, Joan suggested they try washing it out with water, and after several dousings the drowned intruder was extricated.

Then they tried to settle down for the night. Because of the drop to the ground they were forced to be even closer together so those on the outside of the platform wouldn't fall. As they lay in the darkness Betty and Carolyn got to talking about the tribespeople. Wondering how they were faring under the North Vietnamese.

"This past week was to have been the young people's conference at Banmethuot," Betty noted, "also the Bible school program and graduation. I'm sure none of that was allowed. Do you think they are being allowed to meet at all?"

"I wish I knew," Carolyn sighed into the darkness. "I hope they know we are praying for them."

"I wonder about the Christians at home," Betty commented.

"What do you mean?"

"Well, I'm sure they are praying for us, but I wonder if they will also uphold our brothers and sisters in the Lord that we have had to leave."

"Oh, I hope so," Carolyn sniffled. "It means so much to me to know we are being prayed for. And they need that strengthening, too. Maybe even more than we do. There's no telling what they are having to face. Some might not even be alive."

Carolyn was now glad for the night for it hid the tears she could no longer control. In their cramped quarters it was obvious to all the others that she was crying, but no one said anything.

"You know what?" she asked, no longer trying to hide her crying. "It really works."

"What works, Honey?" John inquired comfortingly.

"You really do get tears in your ears when you lie on your back and cry."

Dalat School. Girls' dormitory and students' building at left is original building.
Photo by W.D. Carlsen

Archie and Betty Mitchell, "Mom" and "Dad" to missionary kids (MKs) at Dalat School.

Handyman Archie Mitchell, friend to scores of MKs, examines camera as Mary Frances Holton and Dawnelle Sawin watch.
Photo by W.D. Carlsen

(Below) Betty Mitchell and MKs during story time at Dalat School in 1958.
Photo by W.D. Carlsen

Archie Mitchell leads Dalat MKs in prayer. Many of these young people are now missionaries themselves.
Photo by W.D. Carlsen

Betty Mitchell serving MKs at Dalat School in 1958.
Photo by W.D. Carlsen

6

Hurts and Heartaches

The first of April. Almost three weeks since the group had been discovered by the North Vietnamese at the USAID compound. Yet the sounds of the gongs, the dreary, monotonous diet, and the smells of the prison camp were already familiar. If only they had some inkling of how long they would be held, their captivity would have been easier to bear. But they didn't, and they were getting discouraged.

The new "house" leaked. They had less room and no more protection from the elements than the old hut had provided. Various sleeping positions were devised, but there was just no way everyone could sleep comfortably in the small space.

Even the new eighteen-hole latrine had proven a disappointment. It was totally inadequate to service the thousand-plus residents of the camp. Because a male had to "tiptoe through the tulips" to get to a hole, Peter dubbed it the Tulip Patch. The women still suffered the indignity of using the old two-hole facility which offered no hint of privacy.

To make matters worse each in turn came down with a variety of ailments related to insufficient diet and exposure to the dampness that had settled in with the arrival of the rainy season. Both John and Carolyn suffered excruciating stomach cramps, and Carolyn developed an upper respiratory infection. She became so weak she had to be helped to the latrine. LuAnne had a severe cold and was running a fever. Dick, who had been at the point of physical collapse before capture, could barely stand alone. The others were in only slightly better condition.

They were thankful for having two capable nurses, but when Lil awoke with a cold and chills, the full responsibility of caring for the sick fell on Joan. The camp medic came by and gave John and Carolyn vitamin shots, but he had no medicine to share with prisoners. Fortunately, Paul had a few things left in his survival kit.

The missionaries could not help comparing their circumstances to those of Hank Blood and Betty Olsen. The Bible translator and nurse had died not from torture or injuries, but from malnutrition and untreated illnesses on the trail. Could they expect a similar fate? The thought of having to watch their group die one by one was a horrible prospect.

Carolyn blacked out a couple of times from congestion in her lungs. "I don't think I'll make it," she whispered painfully to Lil.

"Oh, but you have to," her friend assured, still shaking with chills herself. "You have three children waiting for you. You can't let them down."

Finally realizing how sick some of the foreigners were, the camp medic allowed a POW doctor to pay a visit. The POW gave streptomycin and Vitamin B and C shots. This helped Carolyn over her crisis, but her hacking cough continued.

"We must keep our minds distracted, or we'll all crack," Dick warned.

"Listen to the voice of experience," Jay said sarcastically.

"Oh, but he has had experience," Lil rushed to Dick's defense. "His family was in a Japanese prison camp during World War II."

"Really?" Jay replied, now interested.

"Yes, his parents were missionaries in Chinese territory taken over by the Japanese. And they—you tell the story, Dick."

"We Americans were picked up when Pearl Harbor was attacked and repatriated about a year and a half later in an exchange of prisoners." Dick stopped as if that were enough.

"Was it like this?" Paul wondered.

"Oh, there were similarities. An excellent book was written by one of the prisoners, Langdon Gilkey. *Shantung Compound* is the title. Actually, we were only in Shantung a short time, but, yes, the experience was similar.

"Group living is always difficult under crowded conditions," Dick added. "We really do need some diversions; that's why I made the Scrabble game."

It was obvious Dick didn't want to pursue his World War II experience. Jay divided up the Scrabble tiles which Dick had made from cardboard and got out the checkered and numbered board. They played. Everybody played. And to their surprise they enjoyed themselves and began to unwind emotionally, even though their captors thought their games a bit strange.

A source of more amusement to the foreigners was "Sergeant Zero." This cross-eyed noncom could seemingly do nothing right. He was a scream the way he took prisoners to bathe.

First, he would line up a group of Vietnamese prisoners by the gate of the fence that encircled the camp. When he called them to attention they dropped their soap and ragged clothing intended for washing. "Count off," he'd yell. "One, two, three . . ." they'd intone in a high pitch. Then the first prisoner in line had to make a head count. While Zero was checking to see if the count coincided, another prisoner would run up and join the group, making the count wrong.

They'd count over and a prisoner might forget his number, or even call out the number he had the first time, and the tally would be off again. Zero would fume and fuss, while his audience back at the foreigners' hut howled and held their sides—always making sure the frustrated sergeant wasn't looking.

This fiasco might be repeated up to five times. " 'Hogan's Heroes' was never like this," Norm exploded after they had laughed themselves into exhaustion. "Nobody could make such a character believable."

But since the prisoners were allowed only a half hour at the river, they often were robbed of their daily bath.

A more joyful diversion was LuAnne. None of the prisoners would have chosen her to share their misfortune, but she was a blessing to have along. Entertaining LuAnne was an excellent pastime, whether it was telling her *Dew Drop* stories, creating primers in little notebooks to teach her to read, or just smiling over her fantasies.

One evening as the sun was about to sink behind the tree line, John stood up, stretched, and announced, "Well, I guess I'll make one last trip up that lonely trail," and started toward the latrine.

"Wait for me, Daddy," LuAnne called, running to catch his hand. When they reached the facilities, she looked up and smiled, "I don't need to go. I just came so you wouldn't be lonesome."

As they were walking back hand in hand, she lifted her cherubic face and said solemnly, "You know, Daddy, even if I hadn't come with you, you wouldn't have been lonely. Jesus is always with you." John shared her bit of childlike wisdom with the others and they all felt comforted.

Much of the time was spent talking. About their children, their families, their aspirations for the future, and always—food.

They knew they weren't getting the same food as the guards. The *bo doi* were catching fish by throwing grenades into the river. But when the foreigners complained about rice twice a day, the guards would say, "Well, we'll just be hungry together."

They had been on a rice diet for so long that they had begun dreaming about food and spent a great deal of time discussing what they would eat after release.

"I'd settle for a nice juicy hamburger with everything on it," Joan contemplated.

"Just to be free to jump in the car and go out and buy some Dunkin' Donuts and coffee would be great," Norm grinned, smacking his lips at the thought. "When I stop to think how many nights we've lived under curfews and had to stay stuck in the house . . ."

"You remember to tell that to our churches when we get home," Lil suggested.

"No way!" the Canadian vowed. "If I ever get out of here alive and back home, I'll never mention this experience. No way are they going to get me on speaking tours where I have to relive the past few weeks. It's just been too hard."

"Well, something I've learned, that few Americans ever learn, is to be grateful for little things that are usually taken for granted," Carolyn mused. "Like soap. Our last sliver is gone. From now on we'll just have to rinse off and try to stay downwind of each other."

"And toilet paper," added Betty. "And being able to have your hair done."

"Razor blades," John emphasized, pawing at his scratchy

jaws. He and Dick had once tried a cold-water, no-soap shave with a blade the camp commander had given them with a beneficent smile. The blade felt as if every other POW in camp had already scraped his face with it and they gave it up as hopeless.

Ike, who had been listening quietly to the wishing session, poured a ration of powdered milk in hot water he had been boiling. "Shall we have some hot milk before turning in?" There were nods all around and they all enjoyed the warm, sweetened beverage before bedding down in their cramped quarters.

Although the days continued to be tinged with boring monotony, there were continuing reminders of the war still raging in the country. When the drone of a plane was heard, all fires had to be doused instantly, and any white or light-colored clothing that might be draped around had to be pulled in.

More frequently they had to endure the humiliation of inspection by curious Communist officials who came by the camp. The zoolike atmosphere created by the cold stares of visiting officers was dehumanizing, but each time Betty would ask about Archie.

"He was taken prisoner with another male and a woman doctor," she explained. "Have you seen or heard of them?" Each time the reply was negative.

One "inspector" asked Happy which woman belonged to which man, and then, "Where is this woman's husband?" indicating Betty. "Oh, he's dead," was the reply.

"How's that?" Betty demanded. "Do you know that for a fact? Have you heard anything definite?"

"Well, no," the officer admitted. "But it has been so long . . ."

"Well, I don't know that he's dead," Betty declared. "And until I get proof otherwise, I'll keep looking."

Hurts and Heartaches / 103

But there was no news of Archie. What news of the outside world they did get came from two sources. A Raday man who had been captured reported two Christians whom the missionaries knew well had been killed by a grenade. Radios had been confiscated, he said, and there was much fear and mistrust in the villages. But the Christians were still permitted to meet on Sunday mornings for church services. Any other meetings had to be held in homes.

The other news source was Radio Hanoi. Many of the officers had radios which they kept tuned in. When the fall of another South Vietnamese city or province was announced, they would gleefully tell the camp, and the POWs were expected to cheer.

"Qui Nhon has been liberated," the loudspeaker declared, and an obedient chorus of hoorays echoed across the stockade.

"Tuy Hoa has been liberated by our glorious fighters for freedom," and the prisoners likewise responded.

"Nhatrang . . ."

"Nhatrang!" Carolyn gasped, the words choking in her throat. "Our children are in Nhatrang! John, oh, John" she cried, turning to her husband for comfort. But he was too overwhelmed to give much solace.

"Surely they were evacuated," Betty said.

The Millers held on to this hope.

Throughout this time there had been no letup in the interrogations. One by one, day after day, the men were taken out for grilling, with only a break for lunch. Along with the questioning, they were subjected to lectures about the crimes Americans had supposedly perpetrated on the Vietnamese people. Atrocities. Perversions. "And now they are kidnapping babies from Saigon."

The foreign POWs discussed the news of the baby lift. Jay agreed with their captors that it was kidnapping. Paul considered the rescue flights humanitarian efforts. John and Carolyn were less interested in this argument than they were in the possibility that their own children might be among those being flown out of the country. John theorized that if their three oldest had been evacuated from Nhatrang to Saigon, they were probably now being put on one of the planes carrying children from the capital. The possibility was encouraging.

Illness kept plaguing them. Lil's fever jumped to 103 degrees. Norm's sinuses became badly infected and his fever rose also. Dick grew increasingly weaker until Norm asked Joan, "He's not going to make it, is he?" The sad shake of her head indicated that his nurse wife also expected Dick to be the first to die.

The loudspeaker blared the news of another victory. "Today Dalat was liberated from the imperialist forces!" And the cheers rang out.

Betty sat thinking about the many happy years she and Archie had spent there with missionary children. So vivacious and full of life. But they had been good kids, and she had never begrudged the two terms devoted to the children's home. Now some of them were second- and even third-generation missionaries. Others, such as her Becki and David, were preparing. The time had been well invested.

The thought of Becki and David was reassuring. It seemed they had known each other all their lives. They had attended the Dalat School together, but had not fallen in love until later. Dear David who, with his brothers and sisters, carried the legacy of parents martyred at Tet '68. And Becki—would she also carry such a legacy? Betty closed her eyes and prayed silently for David and Becki who were bound for suffering Cambodia, he as a missionary doctor and she a nurse.

Besides having beautiful memories of their children, Betty and the three missionary couples were also thankful for having their Bibles. As time dragged on, they spent more and more

Hurts and Heartaches / 105

time reading and reflecting on Scripture.

The missionaries had never had the time to just read the Bible. With no pressures to do other work, no phones, no interruptions, they read and read. "It's really great," John remarked upon finishing the book of Isaiah at one sitting.

"Well, I just wish you religious people would get off your duffs and help gather firewood," Paul complained irritably.

Norm's dander was up. "What do you mean?" he countered defensively. "We're willing to help, but you guys just take over everything. You think you can do it so much better that we just figured, okay, we'll let you do it."

"I say it's high time to delegate some of the responsibilities around here," Peter chimed in.

"Fine," John agreed. "But while we're clearing the air about our disagreements I'd like to bring up the language that is sometimes used in front of these women, and particularly LuAnne. There's no excuse for it."

"That's right," Norm added, getting quite agitated. "I've heard enough foul language to last the rest of my life. And I'm sure the women agree."

"Yes," Lil admitted in her soft, usually meek voice. "It really hurts me to hear the Lord's name used in vain." The other women gave tight-lipped concurrence.

"Okay," Jay offered, "I'll watch my language if you guys will go easy on *Anthony Adverse*. I really don't think it's necessary to use a whole page of the book every time you go to the head. We could tear the pages in quarters and it'll last a lot longer."

"Well, a quarter of a page might be all right for you men," Lil spoke up, "but we women need more."

"We could settle that dispute easy enough," Peter suggested. "We'll just let you tear out pages of your Bibles to use."

The desecration implied by that remark stung deeply. Lil

burst into tears, and Betty turned her back, not trusting herself to reply.

The squabbles weren't always between missionaries and nonmissionaries. Sometimes Peter and Paul would argue about how best to do a thing; this usually wound up with Peter going off to sulk, while Paul would promptly forget the whole incident. Ike would take orders from Paul, who had been his boss back in Banmethuot, but resented anyone else telling him what to do. Jay spent most of his time visiting the Vietnamese prisoners or else sleeping.

And the missionaries had their hassles, too. Once when Lil asked Carolyn for another needle she was met with a frown.

"What do you do with all those needles, Lil? I don't have an endless supply, you know."

"Well, I gave the last one to one of the Vietnamese prisoners. They don't have anything, and I just wanted to share."

"You keep sharing like that and soon we won't have anything ourselves."

"I don't understand you missionaries," Jay butted in. "I sometimes wonder if you even like the Vietnamese people. Are 'things' really all that important to you?"

Carolyn flushed with shame. "You're right, Jay, of course. I'm sorry. But please have a little patience. Just because we're Christians and missionaries doesn't mean we're perfect. I'll try to be more generous."

Jay's own convictions were tested shortly after when someone stole his sandals down by the river. But he merely shrugged and said, "Well, I guess they needed them more than I did." From then on he went barefoot.

One matter the foreigners agreed on, they would keep their arguments among themselves and always present a united front to the NVA. Living in such crowded, miserable conditions made it inevitable that conflicts would surface within the group. The missionaries, wanting to present an effective wit-

Hurts and Heartaches / 107

ness before their friends, determined to rise above petty annoyances, and they resolved to watch their attitudes more closely.

When they were asked to sign requests for release they were encouraged and decided to try to get letters out to their families. One of the officers took the letters and said he would "try" to mail them. They weren't overly confident that they would ever leave the camp, but thought it wouldn't hurt to try. Betty had given paper and pencils to dozens of Vietnamese POWs and mail within the country was being delivered.

Then came the devastating news of the crash of the C-5A transport carrying 243 children and 62 adults. "Our kids could have been on that plane," Carolyn wept. "And we were happy about the airlift. Now . . . Oh, if we only knew."

"And not just our own children," John added sadly. "Any number of Wycliffe kids from the Nhatrang school could have been on board. Our Wycliffe personnel must have been helping with the evacuation. Chances are we knew some of the victims, even if ours weren't on it."

Fears that the Millers' older three youngsters and other Wycliffe children might have been on the ill-fated plane caused petty differences to fade into insignificance. After a time of trying to console the Millers, the others began to lament their own children.

"I'll tell you what really eats me," Paul said. "My family is safe in Thailand. I know that. And I'm sure glad. But I'm missing so much of my son's first year. I really resent that."

"Yes," Betty sympathized. "They stay little such a very short time. That first year is so precious. I keep thinking of my grandchild. Wondering what she has learned. How big she is.

"And I'm concerned about Gerry. I just trust her brother and sisters are writing to her faithfully. I know this is difficult for her. Especially this coming weekend, for I was planning on being with her."

"And our kids are going to run out of presents," Lil sighed.

"Presents?" Peter puzzled.

"Well, see, the night before they left for school I stayed up and wrapped little gifts for them. One for each Sunday they were gone from us. As love gifts. Just reminders.

"I remember how tired I was that night, but I've been thankful that I did it, because even though our weekly letters have stopped coming they still had the presents to open. But they are all gone now. Betty was going to take a new supply with her this weekend."

"Yeah, it's going to be a long weekend at Dalat School all right," Joan agreed. "A lot of the parents will be visiting. Of course, our kids might have been sent home by now. They might not even be there."

"Oh, I don't think they would have done that yet," Lil said. "They'll let them at least finish this school term. If only we would be released before then . . ." and she couldn't continue.

Betty and Joan decided to walk down to the river.

"I guess I've been especially close to my kids since their father has been gone," Betty explained. "And Gerry has been such a blessing to me. I hate to think of her being alone this weekend. You know how she was with me after Archie was taken."

"Not really," Joan admitted. "Sometimes people tend to forget that we're first-termers. We don't really know all the details of what happened during the sixties."

"Well, I still remember that evening as if it were yesterday," Betty recalled as they sat down by the gnarled roots of a huge tree that shaded the river. She stared silently into the swirling, brown water for a time and then she confided her memories.

"We were really excited about Archie's being appointed superintendent of the Leprosy Control Program. It meant our learning Raday and sharing God's love with the pitiful, maimed tribespeople who come to the leprosarium. And there was a nice, separate house on the grounds for us to live in. The living room had a fireplace with a mantle and bookcases along the sides. There was a roomy screened porch in front.

"We moved in just before Gerry's fourth birthday. The first things Archie unpacked were her tricycle and little rocking chair. He wanted her to feel at home in the new house. Then we unpacked the rest and he helped me hang pictures and put up curtains. Archie always helped me put up curtains.

"We had lived there only a few weeks when it happened. I was in the kitchen doing supper dishes when I heard Ruth Wilting's footsteps going by. She and Dan Gerber were taking a stroll before dark. She must have had on her new red shoes that had a little heel because I could hear the sound so clearly. Everyone usually wore rubber thongs and you couldn't hear them; maybe that's why I remember that so distinctly.

"Ruth was a nurse at the leprosarium. She had recently become engaged to Dan, a conscientious objector who had come out under the Mennonite Central Committee to help the tribespeople with agriculture. It was a lovely evening for a walk.

"Becki was in the living room with Archie, working on her stamp collection. I had already put Gerry to bed early because we were planning on driving into Banmethuot the next day. She had fallen right to sleep. Glenn and Loretta were getting ready for bed. I had gone in their bedroom to help them. Glenn had his pajama bottoms on, and Loretta was wearing shortie pj's. Archie had just called them into the living room to read to them when I heard this sound. Like walking on hard ground.

"I thought at first it must be Ruth and Dan coming back from their walk. Then people started yelling. I couldn't understand what they were saying, but knew it was in Raday. It sounded strange, people yelling in front of our house. I stopped and listened. They yelled it again, and before we even had time to think whether it was a command or what, they came to the door.

"For some reason the screen porch door was hooked, but they just cut through the screen, opened the door, and came in. I could hear these people coming in, but I still couldn't believe it was the Viet Cong. I was shocked. And I know Archie was, too.

"He told the kids, 'Go to your mother,' and they came running. They could see the guns and bayonets and that scared them. Becki ran past me into her room where Gerry was, and Glenn and Loretta stood there by me.

"The VCs started tying Archie up and then they motioned for me to come over by him. Glenn and Loretta scooted into the bathroom and locked the door. They took Archie out the back door and then led me out, too. They didn't have enough rope to tie both of us so they cut off a piece of rope from a hand mop and started to tie me, too. I could hear others in the house trying to get the kids out of the bathroom.

"Archie pleaded with them in Vietnamese, 'Don't take her. Let her stay with the children.' And someone off on the sidelines said, 'No, she's not the one we want.' You see, they had this all planned. They knew exactly what they were doing. The woman they wanted was Dr. Ardel Vietti.

"Well, the kids were yelling, 'They're trying to open the door, what shall we do?' I told them to open the door and come out with me. They came fast. The three older ones.

"The VCs were leading Archie away. We could only call out that we loved him and would be praying for him. He called back, 'That's what you should do.' They didn't even let me kiss him goodbye. They just took him off into the dusk. I remember worrying because he wasn't wearing his hat. He always wore one because he burned very easily and would get a headache if exposed to too much sun.

"They started to lead us off, and I said, 'I want to go back into the house to get my baby.' And they answered, 'No, no. Sorry.' And I pleaded, 'Please, please. I want to get my baby. Why can't I go get her?' So finally one of them said, 'Oh, all right.'

"I hurried up the steps after Gerry, but there were two VCs there and they ordered, 'Get out! You are not supposed to be in here! I told them I just wanted to get her. But they said they wouldn't hurt her, to leave. They pushed me out and raised a bayonet so I couldn't get to her.

"I heard Ruth calling me. I answered, and she came running around the corner of the house and said they had taken Dan, too. They had tied Dan and Archie together and sent her back.

"It was getting dark by this time; the lights in the leprosarium had come on, and the lights in our house were on, too. They led us off toward the nurses' home, and we saw Ardel, our doctor. She was limping badly from an ulcer on her shin, and there were three VCs with her.

"We told her Archie and Dan had been taken and that we were praying. She said, 'All right.' That's all she said, and walked on.

"Then a VC came and asked for the keys to our Land Rover, and I thought, 'That will be better. They'll be able to ride.' Archie had on good walking shoes and could have made it on a trail, but I knew Ardel couldn't with that sore leg.

"They moved us into an area in front of the nurses' house. The children were so quiet. Kind of bewildered looking. After a while we sat down on the ground. Our guards didn't seem to mind. The others were searching through the buildings. Looking for the payroll or medicines, we supposed. We saw them leaving with Ruth's radio, but then they brought it back and said they hadn't taken anything from our houses.

"We sat there a long time. Seemed like a couple of hours,

but it wasn't quite that long. So we sang. This seemed to calm the children, and it helped us, too. I remember singing, 'The Lord Knows the Way Through the Wilderness,' and a number of other choruses.

"Then they started lecturing us. In Raday, so I didn't understand them. One of the girls tried to translate for me, but they said to tell me later. After the lecture they said we were to return to our houses and could sleep there that night, but that we must leave the next day and never come back.

"We hurried back to Gerry. The house was a mess. All the books had been pulled out of the bookcase, the curtains had been jerked off the windows, and bottles and glasses and stuff were all over the table. I dashed through those rooms and found my baby sitting in the middle of the bed. 'Mommy, there were some bad people in our house,' she said.

"I held her close and tried to comfort her. I told her, 'Oh, they weren't so bad. They didn't take the sheets off your bed.' But they had taken all the other sheets and rummaged through our things. So Gerry just smiled, 'Oh, they were good people. They helped us unpack.'

"And they had unpacked all right. They'd taken dishes, bowls, cups, pots and pans, all the linen and curtains, some material I had on my sewing machine, clothes, clock, cameras, knives. Anything they felt would be useful. But in the living room, in the middle of all the debris they had strewn around, I found my Bible. The one Archie had given me on our first trip to Vietnam.

"It was open to Zechariah. I picked it up and the first thing on the page was the second part of chapter nine, verse twelve. It said, 'Ye prisoners of hope.' That was the Lord's message to me then, and it must be for us now, too, Joan. We, too, are 'prisoners of hope.'"

The younger woman placed an understanding hand on Betty's arm and nodded.

Hurts and Heartaches / 113

"The next morning we packed a couple of suitcases and left. One of the VCs had said they would not keep them long so I thought Archie might come back and be worried when he found us gone. I wrote a note and put it on the mantle where he would see it.

"We went into Banmethuot to wait for Archie's release. That was May 31. The day before our fifteenth anniversary. I really expected to see him walking out of the jungle any time. But the days wore on and the older children had to return to school. I was so thankful for Gerry. She was such a comfort to me. I don't know how I would have made it through those long days without her.

"But at night after she was asleep I'd sometimes feel too lonely to go to bed. I'd sit in my rocking chair and sing. Sing and cry and pray. And the Lord was very precious to me at those times. Without Him I could never have stood all the lonely nights since Archie was taken.

"And you know, since we've been captured, I've missed him more than ever. I keep thinking that he is near. In a camp similar to this one, and maybe we'll soon be reunited. Over the years I've learned to withhold my enthusiasm over new rumors, new hopes. But now, I believe more than ever that we'll be together soon."

"Just how long has it been, Betty?"

"Nearly thirteen years. For thirteen long years I've waited for him to come walking out of these jungles back to me. And now I've entered the jungle and can look for him."

Dr. Ardel Vietti with Larry Ward, then of World Vision, in Vietnam and (upper right) ministering to a leper at the Banmethuot leprosarium. (Below right) Dan Gerber, captured along with Ardel Vietti and Archie Mitchell in 1962. Their whereabouts is still unknown.

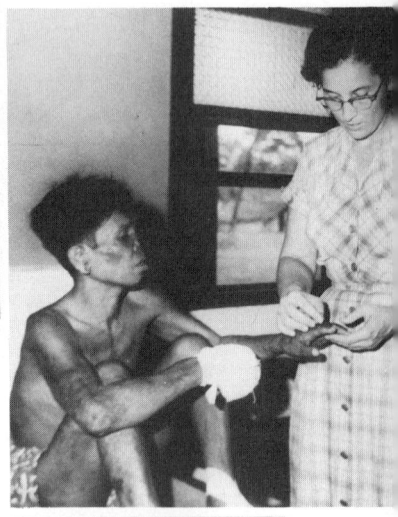

The Mitchell children in Raday dress a few years after their father's capture. (L. to r.) Becki, Gerry, Loretta, and Glenn. (Below) Archie Mitchell at Dalat in 1958 with children Becki, Glenn, and Loretta.

Lepers arriving at Banmethuot leprosarium shortly before the missionaries were captured in 1962.

7

"Camp Wilderness"

In the tiniest script possible Betty made her diary entry for the day: *Long weekend at Dalat School. Thought I'd be with my daughter today. But God has ordered a different plan. Be very, very near Gerry, dear God, I pray. And all my dear children.*

The other mothers were lonely, too, as they sat in the thatched hut trying to reassure one another.

"It does help to know mine are being well cared for," Lil sighed gratefully, "that Charlotte and Woody Stemple are there as houseparents. They know what it means to be separated from their kids."

"Yes," Betty affirmed. "Gerry's with dear friends who have known and loved her all her life. Her 'aunties' couldn't love her more if she really were their niece. And the Manghams, her houseparents, understand, too. Ed was one of mine and Archie's kids at the old Dalat School."

Lil smiled at Joan, who had been listening quietly. "Your

two are with ours. They're fine."

"I know. But my Pat and Doug weren't born on a mission field and raised always knowing there would be periods of separation from their parents. It must be harder for them."

"Oh, but your kids have adjusted well," Lil assured her.

"Yes," Betty agreed. "They always seemed to fit right in with the others."

"That's true," Joan realized. "Maybe it's just their mother who has a hard time adjusting to the separation."

Carolyn sat silently, her face turned away. Not knowing quite what to say to her, the others continued talking among themselves.

"It's hard for all of us," Lil continued. "But at least I can work on butterflies. My kids are out of presents now, but working on a new collection to replace the one I had to leave makes me feel a little closer to them."

Lil carefully dated a new addition that one of the Vietnamese POWs had caught for her. Carefully she wrapped the brightly colored insect with a slice of plastic from Betty's suitcase and gently placed it in one of the tiny medicine boxes cajoled from the camp medic.

By this time the foreigners were adept scavengers. Any loose scrap of paper, plastic, metal, or wire was quickly appropriated and put to practical use. Even LuAnne kept a sharp eye out for any potentially useful item. She would spot a piece of string or a rubber band and run gleefully to her mother with her treasure.

The next day, April 12, was special. They enjoyed fish juice with their *chao* for breakfast and Peter made "rice coffee" by browning fresh rice until almost black, then boiling it to produce a drinkable liquid. In the evening they cooked some leaves for greens and were delightfully surprised when the guards presented a batch of fresh deer meat.

Just sinking their teeth into something was almost as much a treat as tasting the delectable protein. They cut their portions into small bites and chewed each morsel slowly, savoring the flavor. It wasn't easy, but they forced themselves to save some for the next day.

A couple of days later the food situation looked even brighter when a contingent of *bo doi* returned from a village market. The prisoners were allotted some dried pork, sugar, and one can of milk and were permitted to purchase a bag of peanuts, soap, toothpaste and brushes, tobacco for the smokers, and some real coffee. Items taken for granted before captivity now seemed like luxuries—even the soap that smelled as if it had just come from a tannery.

Norm roasted the peanuts and they sprinkled some on their rice. The crunchy, nutty flavor made the daily portions of grain more palatable. "Wonder why the good food?" he mused. "Are they fattening us for the kill, or do you think they might be getting ready to let us go?"

"The American POWs released in '72 said they got better treatment just before being repatriated," Dick recalled.

"I'll try to get some information from the grunts," Norm decided. He went over to one of the guards with whom he had become friendly and who was continually listening to Radio Hanoi. Norm would teasingly suggest he tune in BBC or ABC, so he was called Mr. ABC or Mr. BBC.

The tall Canadian came back from his discussion all smiles. "We may be going on a trip!"

Speculation began about where they might be going and why. They hoped they would be taken to Loc Ninh, the old provisional capital north of Saigon, and released from there.

LuAnne's sore throat became worse that night, her fever soaring to almost 105 degrees. Her mother and the nurses took turns sponging to bring her temperature down. In the morning the medic gave her some medicine and diagnosed her illness as extremely infected tonsils.

Jay was sick also and was given some medicine. It appeared to the nurses, though, that standard procedure for treating the sick in the prison camp was to give just enough medicine to ward off fatalities, but not enough to really cure anyone. Carolyn still had her hacking cough, Dick wobbled weakly, and Paul was speckled with methiolate from doctoring various self-inflicted cuts and scratches.

Then a new political officer was added to the cast of characters—"Mr. Spectacles," named for the obvious reason. About 5:00 A.M. he officially informed them, "You will be moving to a new and better camp."

"What will our status be there?" Norm inquired impatiently. "We keep getting different opinions as to whether or not we are prisoners of war. Just where do we stand? We'd really like to know."

"The answer to that question, Mr. Johnson, depends on the results of our research. If we find you are who you say you are, then you are our friends and honored guests. If, however, we find you have been conducting activities that would obstruct our independence and freedom, then you are our prisoners. In the meantime, keep healthy."

After learning they would be moving out Carolyn was hesitant to give LuAnne the penicillin the medic had prescribed. The possibility of a reaction in the back of a truck to medication she had not taken before forced her to withhold the drug. She prayed they would not again be subjected to another seven-hour test of endurance on the road.

As they packed their gear the pulses of the prisoners quickened. Norm was excited. He really expected they would be released. When he could restrain himself no longer he ran up and hugged Mr. ABC and BBC. "Goodbye, we're going home!"

"Camp Wilderness" / 121

After everything was packed and moved to the road, the Millers asked to leave some of their useless paraphernalia behind. They were told, "No, all must go."

Finally, at 8:20 A.M., a big Russian-made truck lumbered up. They were told they would ride with the Vietnamese sick and wounded.

Except for Peter and Jay. "Mr. Whitlock and Mr. Scarborough will not go at this time," Spectacles announced.

Having to leave the two fellows upset the rest of the group. Despite their differences, they had developed a deep sense of loyalty to one another.

"Do not worry," Spectacles assured. "They will be joining you later. In the meantime, keep happy."

The rest began climbing on board. The truck was cramped but not as badly as last time. Still Carolyn hung back until a guard took pity and told her she could sit up front and hold her sick daughter.

As they bounced along in the truck, it was too noisy to talk. Most of their thoughts ran on a similiar track: Where are we going? What will happen to us? Will we really be released? Only Betty was thinking: Are they taking us to Archie? Will my years of waiting soon be over?

Hour after weary hour the old truck chugged northward along the Ho Chi Minh Trail, the old supply line for North Vietnamese troops and supplies coming south. Because of the heavy war use, this road was not as bumpy as the previous one. Inside the cab, crowded with five people, LuAnne slept while Carolyn sat cramped and sore. With each kilometer, Carolyn felt the bony child become heavier and heavier on her lap.

After a long weary day of traveling the driver braked to a stop and the prisoners were ordered out. Betty peered at her watch under the truck's headlights. Nine o'clock. Pitch dark. They appeared to be in the middle of a wilderness, penetrable only by the road on which they had come.

"We walk from here," a voice declared. Sweaty and droopy, the disappointed prisoners picked up their belongings and started trekking into the jungle. It was clear they were not being taken to a repatriation center.

The Millers felt they could no longer carry all their possessions. Without asking permission, they left the big brown suitcase containing dishes and other equipment and the portable sewing machine on the side of the road. Then they fell into line.

Sick and wounded, weak and weary, the foreign and Vietnamese POWs stumbled along single file. The guards interspersed among them attempted to point the way by flashlights. On and on they marched into the darkness with leaves and branches stinging them in the face. They slid down into pitch black ravines and then crawled back up the other side, while the guards with lights picked their way over foot logs. It became impossible to stay close to one another.

"Help me! Oh, please help me!" came a quavering cry.

"A snake has Lil!" Norm feared, as he ran stumbling back toward the sound of her voice.

"Ants!" Lil screamed. "Fire ants. Crawling all over me." She was pounding her body, trying desperately to kill the tormenting insects. Norm tried to knock off as many as possible.

"Move on!" Dick commanded as he caught up with them, "or more will get on you."

They stomped off, slapping at the ants as they went.

"How long will this last?" Lil wailed.

"No telling," Dick replied. "But we have to speed up or we'll be lost from the others."

The jungle showed no promise of thinning out as they slugged along the narrow trail. When the Millers came upon the ant hill LuAnne screamed as ants climbed her bare legs.

John and Carolyn had been struggling under the weight of their remaining belongings. "This is ridiculous," John snorted as he dropped a heavy bag and picked up his sobbing youngster. "Don't cry, Sweetheart. Daddy will carry you."

Carolyn added the bag to her already heavy load and they stumbled on into the darkness, placing one foot before the other, unsure of what they would step into next.

A half hour or so later they heard brush crackling. Looking back, they saw lights bobbing. Several NVA soldiers pushed by, one carrying the Millers' big brown suitcase. Slung on a pole between two others was the useless electric sewing machine.

Then just when they thought the march would never end, the lights ahead suddenly stopped. Coming up behind the soldiers, the prisoners saw the ghostly outline of a longhouse in a tight clearing. Debilitated almost to the verge of collapse, they somehow managed to scramble onto the sleeping platforms that ran along the sides of the thatch-roofed hut. Flopping down in a helter-skelter manner, they soon dropped off into exhausted slumber.

They awoke to a wet, drippy dawn and the loud clanging of a gong. This "nicer" camp was even more primitive than Camp Sunshine. The jungle grew right up to the sides of the longhouse. Although this was hilly jungle near the Cambodian border, the humidity and dampness made it obvious that it was lower in altitude.

"Boy, this is a real hideaway," John observed. "We're so deep in the jungle no one could ever find us."

"Do you think they'll really bring Peter and Jay here?" Norm asked.

"I wouldn't depend on it," Paul replied dejectedly. "I haven't much confidence in anything they tell us anymore."

"Yeah," the Canadian concurred. "I really anticipated we would be released. This place is a big disappointment."

"Yes," Betty murmured softly, "a big disappointment."

The gong clanged again. A guard came over and grunted,

"You work now. Come."

The men were led off to work on the latrines while the women were ordered to straighten up around the longhouse. Joan was acutely aware of the hurt in Betty's voice.

"You've known a lot of disappointments, haven't you?" she asked compassionately.

"Yes," Betty sighed, "but I thought I'd learned not to let my hopes get too high. When Archie was first taken I fully expected him to be released right away. That one VC had said they weren't going to keep him long. So when word would filter out of the jungle from some of the tribespeople that he and Ardel and Dan had been seen here or there, I believed them.

"I always had the feeling that he wasn't too far away. That's why when it came time for us to go back to the States on furlough I decided to stay on."

"How did your kids feel about that?"

"Oh, they were with me. They thought he'd be back with us soon. I remember on Glenn's birthday that year Becki spent the day looking out a window toward the jungle. She thought her daddy would be home to help us celebrate. She wouldn't even come down for the party until after it was dark and she knew her dream wasn't going to come true.

"And they all prayed so hard that he would be with us for Christmas. And then for Easter. His birthday. Our anniversary. Whatever big event was coming up. For his birthday, I baked a pie and the children sang, 'Happy birthday, dear Daddy.'

"Then in November of 1967 I felt so strongly that the Lord was telling me to go home, but to take a furlough then didn't really make sense. The cold weather in Oregon at that time of year would be hard on us, and it was in the middle of a school term for the children. But I had to obey what I felt was the Lord's leading.

"While we were in the States we heard that a captured Viet Cong soldier had seen Archie, Ardel, and Dan alive and that they had been joined by Hank Blood and Betty Olsen. Dr. Bailey, as president of the Alliance, made the announcement at the annual Council of our churches. Everyone was so thrilled and happy. I wondered why the Lord had led me home instead of allowing me to remain in Vietnam where I could have talked to the VC myself.

"Then when the terrible destruction of Tet came, I understood. If I had still been in Banmethuot at that time, I probably would have been killed. You see, Joan, the Lord's timing really is perfect. He does know and has our best interest in mind. Even though I sometimes have to keep reminding myself."

"Yes, but what about that report? Did the VC say Archie was well? Where were they? What—?"

"That report turned out to be another big letdown. We learned when the POWs were released in 1972 that both Hank and Betty were dead before that sighting. The VC either lied or was mistaken."

"Oh," Joan replied softly.

"So there was no need for me to have been in Banmethuot then. See, God really does know best. And even in our present situation we have to keep believing that He 'knows the way through the wilderness.' "

Joan agreed. "Thanks for that reminder, Betty. I really needed it. Today is Doug's fourteenth birthday and Norm and I are feeling low. Especially Norm, since he was so sure we were going to be let go."

"Birthdays are hard," Betty sympathized. "We'll have to really hold up your Doug in prayer today."

"Please do," the lonely mother requested. "If only he might get some word that we're alive and safe, that would be the best present he could have."

Again the gong echoed through the dense forest. Once,

twice, three times. The number of times indicated the particular announcement, but the prisoners didn't know the meaning of the number of gongs at this new camp. They would watch the Vietnamese prisoners and guards and follow suit.

This time it was calling the workers to eat.

As they downed the monotonous rice, Norm started talking about Doug. "He's always been a good kid. Easygoing. A well-rounded athlete. Well-mannered. He has never been a discipline problem for us."

"Yeah, and he's got that cute smile," Carolyn added.

"That's right," Lil agreed. "All the girls like him."

"He even gets along with his sister," Joan put in proudly. "Our kids are only thirteen months apart, but they've always stuck up for one another. Oh, they quarrel sometimes, but when there's a need they band together. I'm just so thankful they're together." Sudden tears welled up and then began spilling down her cheeks. "If only they know that we're all right." Norm put a strong arm around her but couldn't trust himself to say anything. The touching scene was a silent call to prayer for the other missionaries.

From that first day it was apparent that Camp Wilderness, as they termed it, was very different from Camp Sunshine. Not only because of the obvious physical differences of living deep in the moldy jungle, but because this was a work camp.

"We're all here together," an officer explained to them. "We all must eat, so we must work together. Besides, when you are active you are more content." He managed a thin smile, adding, "Sundays will be easier."

There was another reason for working. More prisoners were on the way, camp officials said, necessitating the building of two new longhouses. But first priority would be the digging of latrines, a must for sanitation.

These were simple affairs, but they had to be dug very deep

and the men were in a weakened condition from inadequate food. The foreigners had been asked, but never forced, to do this work, but since it was required of their fellow Vietnamese prisoners they wanted to help. Even Dick pitched in, pushing himself as much as possible.

On Dick's birthday, April 21, Lil placed a red candle in a bowl of rice and they all sang to him. Then they "feasted" on manioc and enjoyed as a special treat roasted peanuts they had been saving.

The manioc was a welcome addition to their diet. They ate both the potatolike roots of the nutritious starchy vegetable and the leaves. They fried leftover rice for a crunchy treat that offered something to chew on. This, along with "rice coffee," topped off the special meal.

After the second rain the latrine that the foreign POWs had tried to shore up collapsed on Betty. As the women helped her out of her embarrassing position, she had the good grace to laugh at herself. The tiny shelter had not been fashioned with the tall American in mind. A lean-to, makeshift outhouse, which the foreign men made by themselves, proved more sturdy. While offering little in the way of privacy, it did have a roof to protect the user from the elements.

The men were also assigned to carry supplies from a storage area some four or five miles distant. There was little semblence of a trail, and when carrying heavy loads back to Camp Wilderness it seemed twice as far. The men would take an extra bag with them and then divide the hundred-pound bags of rice, since none could manage a full bag. Wooden crates of dried fish were carried over their shoulders, while tin cans of grease were attached to ends of a bamboo pole and balanced across their shoulders.

The back-breaking loads forced them to stop often on the way. "How can I possibly carry this any farther," Norm panted one day, "when I can't even pick it up?" The guard helped him position his load on his shoulders once more and he trudged ahead.

Coming back the next time, Norm gasped to Dick, "I'm just not going to make it."

"Take it a step at a time," advised Dick, who was himself groaning under a terrible load.

Somehow Norm did make it and went back again, this time with John. Again, he feared every step would be his last one, but he managed to reach the camp and there collapsed in a heap.

The men who weren't carrying supplies gathered wood to keep their fire going. When they had a pile of reserve fuel, they were ordered to begin cutting away the undergrowth that was threatening to engulf the longhouse. The goal was to clear the jungle fifty feet back in a perimeter around the dwelling. The variety of snakes that inhabited the dense undergrowth spurred them on in this herculean task.

The hard labor, after weeks of inactivity at Sunshine, produced aching backs and sore muscles. But the time did pass more quickly.

Besides cleaning the hut the women were to pick, clean, and prepare the manioc, boil their water, and help with the clearing around the house.

Their favorite time of day was when they were allowed to go to the river alone to bathe. Verdant, flowering vegetation grew right down to the bank of the clear stream. In their secluded section they swam, sunbathed, and often prayed. The scent of wild flowers added to their pleasure.

Lil caught a tiger butterfly on one of their excursions. "Oh, isn't he beautiful?" she exclaimed. "Even in a prison camp they can't hide from us the beauty of God's creation."

They sat in silence just drinking in the sights of the natural paradise. A bird swooped down, caught a fish from the river, and carried it to his cheering mate in a tree across the water. Another butterfly fluttered by, but Lil was feeling too content to chase it. LuAnne was splashing happily in the water nearby. Betty twirled a lavender orchid between her fingers.

"Is it wrong to feel so good about being here?" Lil asked, feeling a little guilty.

The others laughed companionably. "We understand what you mean," Joan smiled.

"Yes," Betty nodded. "It's so peaceful here surrounded by all this beauty that it really does make you feel close to the Lord. If only our families knew we were here."

They returned to the camp to find the men bone tired from pulling stumps from a new house site. Then they received a luscious surprise. A piece of fruit. The first they had eaten since they were captured. It was a kind of wild plum that tasted like a cross between a plum and a quince. Delicious!

The deep jungle surrounding their house kept the setting sun from view, and evening fell sooner than would be expected in late April. They were not required to go to bed until nine o'clock, so in the early hours of the evening they sat around the fire and talked and sang. Ike fashioned some bamboo noisemakers that furnished a rhythmic beat to their harmony.

One evening after Norm returned from a trip to the latrine he nodded toward the deep shadows and whispered to Joan, "We've got an audience."

"Guards?" Joan asked.

Norm nodded affirmatively. "And would you believe I saw the camp commander?"

They were quite surprised that the officer would be listening to their "Blue" songs. The Communists classified all songs as "Red," "Yellow," or "Blue." The preferred Red songs were patriotic communistic melodies. The Yellow were popular ballads such as country and western, but no jazz or rock and roll. These the Communists allowed but generally they did not want to hear hymns or American patriotic songs, which they considered "Blue." That is why the officer, who seldom visited the POWs, was listening in secret.

They had just settled down for the night when a beam of light suddenly flashed in their faces. Norm quickly turned over and recognized "Jumpy," a guard who seemed to take delight in tormenting his charges.

"It is my responsibility to account for you prisoners," the belligerent *bo doi* snapped. "No one will escape while I am on duty!"

"Where could we escape to anyway?" Norm muttered under his breath.

The next day this same ill-tempered guard started an argument with the prisoners. "From now on you will not go to the latrines at will. You will stand at attention and ask permission before going and upon returning."

This seemed totally unnecessary in such a small camp where it was quite obvious to everyone where they were going. To make it even more humiliating he expected them to ask with certain Vietnamese phrases, which he had never bothered to teach them.

"Stand straight," he snapped at Betty, when she had asked permission to use the facilities. "Arms down. And use the correct words."

It took all the control she could muster not to argue with the picky guard. When she returned he made her go through the same routine. Frustrated, she returned to the longhouse and wrote in her diary: *A change in rules for going and returning from the toilet. Lord, help us not to complain.*

She had not forgotten the verses in Philippians claimed when first captured. Her heart's desire was still to be a light among this generation of darkness, but she felt more than ever the need for supernatural strength to keep her end of the bargain and not to murmur or complain.

By the end of the first week in the new camp LuAnne was feeling better and had charmed all the guards except Jumpy who was too miserable to even like himself. The others brought the five-year-old extra food and fruit. Although she enjoyed the treats, she remained shy with the guards and stayed close to her mother. No matter how friendly they tried to be she just couldn't bring herself to trust them, and Carolyn was glad. Being separated from her other three children had made her even more protective of LuAnne than she normally would have been.

On April 29 a long line of foot-weary prisoners began dragging into the camp. Among the first arrivals were Peter and Jay. Accompanied by Mr. Spectacles, they had walked about a hundred kilometers in eight days. Peter's feet were cut quite badly and were very sore. Jay had been issued a pair of Ho Chi Minh sandles—cut from old rubber tires in the shape of feet with straps on them—so he didn't have to walk barefooted, but he had developed a huge boil on his knee.

"I didn't think we'd ever make it," Jay moaned. "That was one looooong walk. And we had to carry our own rice, so the food was pretty scarce."

"It was quite an extraordinary experience," Peter agreed. "And we are only the first of a multitude of marchers that must stretch for several kilometers. An extremely disorganized band."

His estimate was not an exaggeration, for prisoners kept coming all day. By nightfall the population had grown from about forty to almost three hundred. Eleven noncoms who had been billeted with the foreigners were moved out and replaced by South Vietnamese officers. Altogether, there were around eighty POWs in the foreigners' longhouse and about a hundred in each of the two new dwellings.

The foreigners felt good to be together again. Despite theological and philosophical differences Jay and Peter were part of the family, and everyone felt more contented with them there. Besides, their choir seemed incomplete without these two good singers.

Many Vietnamese were also familiar from days at Sunshine. Betty, especially, took every opportunity to witness to the other POWs, sometimes to the displeasure of some of their own group.

"She's a fanatic," Peter griped one day. "If she wants to live her life by blind faith, that's her affair, but does she have to foist her beliefs on others?"

Lil defended her friend. "Her faith in the Lord has seen her through many difficult circumstances, and she shares it with love and concern."

"Ah, you missionaries are always trying to change the people's culture," Paul complained.

"Civilization changes culture more than Christianity," Carolyn countered, and they were off on another discussion.

But while they were arguing Betty had an opportunity to witness to one of the crippled POWs. She was deeply touched when the small man confided he had given his new shoes to a friend because the stronger man was required to do more walking than he.

At noon on April 31 they heard Saigon had surrendered. The required cheer clearly lacked enthusiasm.

Mr. Spectacles reported to the foreigners stories of panic in Saigon as people had tried to evacuate. "They were frightened by propaganda," he explained. "There was no cause for fear."

The missionaries said nothing, wondering silently if their friends and colleagues had escaped.

Mr. Spectacles left.

"At least the fighting is over," Betty sighed in acceptance.

"If America had stayed out of it, the fighting would have been over long ago," Jay sniped.

"Yes, I suppose that's true," the veteran missionary conceded. "But much has been accomplished during the years of American involvement that wouldn't have been otherwise. The Lord's timing is ripe. There are now believers in the various tribes and at least portions of Scriptures and trained leaders. The fall of Saigon may signal the end of missionary work in Vietnam, but it doesn't mean the spread of the gospel will stop."

Her colleagues, who had continued busily with their own thoughts, nodded agreement.

8

Scourge of the Tropics

May Day. No work. A time of feasting and celebration for the Communists and a day of rest for the prisoners. As a special treat they were given an extra ration of manioc, and for LuAnne egg and some meat.

During the night she complained of feeling sick. She rolled and tossed restlessly, saying her legs ached. Carolyn took her temperature: 104 degrees.

Besides the insufficient diet the weather was enough to make anyone sick. During the day when the sun was out it was hot and humid, then with the ever increasing black clouds would come a cold, chilling rain. Carolyn tried to convince herself that LuAnne had only a cold, but underneath was a nagging fear that her five-year-old had been smitten with the scourge of the tropics—malaria.

The next day the sun rose, drawing steam from the thick undergrowth that had been soaked by showers the night before. For the men it was back to work.

"Put your shirts on!" the guard yelled at Peter and Paul who had stripped to the waist. The sun was beating down on them as they swung the long machetes back and forth, and sweat was rolling down their backs.

"Put your shirts on!" he yelled again, making motions to indicate what he meant. Neither Peter nor Paul spoke Vietnamese, but they clearly understood.

"It's too hot!" Peter yelled back in English.

"Everyone must wear shirts," the guard insisted.

"If we have to work this hard, we aren't going to wear shirts," Paul shouted.

The guard couldn't understand English, but knew he wasn't being obeyed. "Shirts on!" he demanded even louder, as if by raising his voice he would be understood.

"No way, it's too hot," Peter and Paul insisted.

The missionaries, who understood both languages, listened in amusement as the verbal battle raged, but at the same time they realized the reason behind the command. The camp officials didn't want the men to be bitten by malaria-carrying mosquitoes.

Inevitably the guard won the battle and oversaw the prisoners putting on their shirts. "It's stupid," Paul grumbled. "We can be bitten on our hands or face. Wearing a shirt isn't going to protect us." As soon as the guard's back was turned they pulled off their constricting garments.

Norm and John returned from another five-mile hike to and from the storage camp, and Norm fell prostrate on the sleeping platform.

"What a trip!" John said, almost completely out of breath. "I didn't know if Norm was going to make it back. I think we're both dehydrated."

The noncom prisoners dressed in black pajamas had begun building a bamboo fence around the perimeter of the camp.

When the foreigners asked about it they were told, "It's for your protection. To keep others away from you."

Already the fence was past the latrines and a bomb crater, and the workmen were now closing off the haven of beauty on the secluded section of river bank where the women went to bathe and pray. Betty, Joan, Lil, and Carolyn were understandably depressed that this one privacy of the day should be denied them. Now they would have to use a more open spot.

Night fell, and a heavy rain pounded the thatch roof which leaked so badly over the single men that Jay opted for spending the night on the ground.

The next morning both Norm and Jay had fevers, Norm's up to 104.8 degrees.

"I'm going to report Norm's symptoms to the medic," Joan declared, and left to get some medicine.

Norm started on quinine, but Jay felt better, his temperature having gone down. So concerned was Joan about her husband's condition that she spent most of the day sponging him, trying to bring down his fever. Finally, she made another trip to the medics to beg for aspirin.

"They either don't have much medicine, or they sure are stingy with it," she reported. "I had to nag and nag to get this." She held out one precious white tablet.

When Betty pulled out her tiny diary to record the events of the day she saw a previous notation: *Banquet before conference starts.*

The annual banquet was the big event of the year for the Alliance missionaries in Vietnam. A time of coming together, seeing friends from different sections of the country. A time of fellowship and rejoicing in accomplishments for the Lord during the previous year.

Her mind raced back to the first conference she had attended after Archie had been taken captive. It had been nearly a year and she missed him deeply, dreading to go to the banquet without him. Her children realized how difficult it was for her, and Becki volunteered to accompany her so she wouldn't have to sit by herself. But sensing this was something she would have to face, she got dressed up, put on a smile, and went alone.

"And people are always saying I'm strong," she thought with a sigh. "If only they knew how very hard it was for me to force myself to go to that banquet."

The next day, Sunday, John led in Bible studies. Norm was still burning with a temperature over 104.5 degrees and that evening they had special prayer for him. During the prayer time Lil also prayed the Lord would heal her leg which was painful and quite swollen. The next morning it was back to normal and Norm was much better, but he continued taking shots.

While John was chopping away undergrowth within the perimeter of the camp he was fretting that Carolyn's birthday was coming in a couple of days and he had no gift for her. So he began praying, "Lord, help me think of something I can make or do so I can encourage Carolyn by making her birthday special." While he was still hacking away he came upon a crusty shell that had been fired from a Cobra gunship.

"Thank you, Lord," he whispered and tried to figure something he could make of it. "I'll just shine it up and she can use it as a toothpick holder, or maybe as a container for her hair clips."

He couldn't find anything to polish it with, but Lil gave him an old piece of Mnong manuscript that she had been tearing up for toilet paper and helped him wrap it as a gift. It wasn't a necklace from Tiffany's, but it was all he could dredge up to express his love.

That evening they sat at the new bamboo table Ike had built and ate fried, dried rice and noodle soup for Carolyn's birthday. Then they sang and John shyly presented his gift.

LuAnne, who was feeling a little better, danced around all excited. Everyone watched as Carolyn opened it with expectancy, genuinely happy to have anything. She tore back the paper to reveal the ugly old shell casing, but she thought it was beautiful, for it was a love gift.

"I'll treasure it always," she exclaimed, holding it tightly.

May 7 marked the end of their eighth week in captivity, with no idea of how much longer they would be held. The fence was up now and most of the cleaning had been done inside, giving the camp a rather stockadelike appearance. But many of the prisoners had strung orchids in the longhouses, an ever present reminder of the loving art of the Creator.

The monsoon season was at its peak and the chilling rain was taking its toll. Having lost a lot of weight and strength, the POWs were going down hill physically. The men found it more and more difficult to carry loads of food, thatch, or bamboo and then to get to their required political lectures in the evening.

Though LuAnne received vitamin shots, her health remained poor. When the frail child managed to take her shot one day without crying Carolyn rummaged through her big suitcase for some kind of treat. She discovered a half stick of gum. LuAnne was delighted. Real gum! She skipped around showing everyone her prize. Deciding she would enjoy it even more if she shared it, she broke off two tiny pieces, one for "Aunt Lil" and one for "Aunt Betty."

All the prisoners were concerned about LuAnne. To see their "little ray of sunshine" waste away was almost more than they could take. The medic mentioned the possibility of sending her to a field hospital and he thought he could arrange for Carolyn to accompany her, but John's going could not be considered.

John and Carolyn wanted LuAnne to receive the best care possible, but the thought of separation was another matter.

They had experienced over two months of separation from their older children and weren't sure they could bear to be separated from each other.

"If they'll let one of the other couples go, I'd agree to it," John said at last. "I don't want you to be alone."

That night Norm's temperature soared to 105 degrees, Lil's to 104.4, and she was wracked with chills. Again, Joan went to beg for more medicine. When she couldn't get any she prayed and debated with herself over what further to do. Finally, that night while the other men were at a "command performance" movie on the "glories" of the revolution, she decided that come morning she would appeal to the camp commander for better treatment for her husband. She wasn't certain what his reaction would be, but she knew that Norm was going to die if something wasn't done quickly.

The men returned with news that a Vietnamese POW had died. "I talked with the camp commander for a few minutes," Peter told Joan. "He asked how we were getting along, and I told him how sick Norm was and that he needed better medical care."

"Thanks, Peter, I really appreciate that," Joan replied. "What did he say?"

"Said he'd be by in the morning to see him."

The missionaries gathered that night for another time of special prayer for the sick. Norm was so bad off he didn't seem to know what was going on and couldn't enter into the prayer time.

The next morning they were given a banana—one banana for twelve people. After two months without the tropical fruit that had been a mainstay during their years in Vietnam their mouths watered as they contemplated a bite of the lovely yellow fruit. Paul divided it into twelve even pieces. One slice apiece. The most delicious banana any of them had ever tasted. Each savored his slice until it melted into the throat.

Scourge of the Tropics / 141

After breakfast Joan was again sponging Norm, trying to get his fever down, when the camp commander arrived. The once husky Canadian looked gaunt and pale. His dark beard made his skin appear all the whiter and his fever made him incoherent.

The commander talked to the prisoners awhile as Joan continued to fuss with Norm, trying to make him more comfortable. Finally the officer said with surprising tenderness, "You really love him, don't you?"

"Oh, yes!" Joan replied, tears filling her eyes.

"Well, we'll have to do something for him. We'll get him to the field hospital. You may accompany him."

Joan rejoiced at the prospect of Norm's receiving better treatment, but the Millers looked at each other desperately. John and Carolyn didn't want to be separated, but they stood by their decision. Since the Johnsons were going, Carolyn and LuAnne would go along.

As Joan and Carolyn packed in preparation for leaving it was decided that Dick, Jay, and John would walk with them the three or four kilometers to the road. Since a truck would be coming to take them to the hospital the Millers concluded it would be best for Carolyn to take most of their things with her. "You never can tell, I might have a mighty long walk to join you," John reasoned.

The path to the road was much easier to navigate during the day than it had been when they had entered nearly a month before. Then, too, it had been trampled down by the influx of prisoners arriving after them. Even so the walk was torturous for Norm who was so weak he could hardly put one foot in front of the other. It was a slow, slow trek.

When they arrived at the Ho Chi Minh Trail the guards told those who were leaving to enter a little house by the roadside. The others were to return immediately. John hugged his wife and daughter, kissed them goodbye, then started back down the trail behind Dick and Jay as fast as he could.

They arrived back at the longhouse after supper, but the others had saved them some food. John couldn't swallow his and walked off from the hut to the bomb crater. The impact of being without Carolyn and LuAnne hadn't really hit him until he got back to the house. He was within a stockade with over three hundred people, but had never felt so alone.

Unashamedly he cried as he prayed for Carolyn and LuAnne who were being driven to some unknown destination. And he prayed for his Margie and Gordon and Nate. Wherever they were. Separated from his whole family, he could only commit them to the Lord's protection and care. That night he had plenty of room under the mosquito net he usually shared with his wife and daughter, but he didn't enjoy it.

Lil was still sick with malaria, and it fell to Betty to nurse her. The years Betty had devoted to assisting with leprosy patients had not earned her a degree, but they had taught her a lot about nursing techniques. Her loving care was rewarded by Lil's improvement.

The next day Betty helped Lil down to the river to bathe in their new location. "I'll have to admit, Lil, that I'm glad you didn't go to the hospital. I sure wouldn't want to be the only woman with all these men."

"I thought of that," Lil replied softly. "I'm feeling some better. If we could just go a couple of days without rain, I believe I'd recover."

They bathed and washed some clothes in the river and then prayed for those who had gone to the hospital and for their children and loved ones at home. The two women had known each other for years, but in the days of trials they had become closer than sisters.

Lil regained strength slowly. Lying down one afternoon resting, feeling rather discouraged, she opened her eyes to see a dazzling butterfly gracing her blanket. Everyone in the camp knew by this time about her collection and even the guards would timidly bring her specimens because she would always smile and thank them profusely. But this butterfly seemed to be a special messenger sent to remind her of God's love. She decided not to try to catch it.

Lil and Betty weren't expected to do as much hard labor as the men, so they had more opportunities to share their faith with the other POWs. The believers came to them for encouragement and the non-Christians listened politely. The guards would always say, "We don't need religion now that the revolution has come." But they entered into discussions nonetheless.

When they were informed they might write to their families the foreigners were overwhelmed. Betty wrote to Gerry in Malaysia and started a letter to Glenn in California before realizing they might make them use some special form. She decided to wait until the next day before writing more.

Lil addressed her letter to her four children at the Dalat School. After writing it she turned to Dick, "How does this sound, Honey? Tell me if I should add anything."

Sunday, May 18, 1975

Dearest, dearest Jeanie, Brian, Ruthie and Johnnie,

We love you very, very much. We hope you are well and happy. We pray for each of you. Remember that God's love is around each of you and around us, too. We still have a snapshot of each of you and we look at them over and over again. We hope and pray we can all be together again soon.

We wonder how you are doing in the dorm and at school. We know many kind people are helping you. Try hard to do your best for Jesus and for us. It will be a great day when you can show us all you have done and tell us all that has happened to you.

All around us we can see how beautiful God has made the world. Beautiful flowers here, especially orchids. Lavender, orange, yellow, and white. I am pressing some for you. There are interesting rocks. I've kept a few. Jeanie, you would like them.

And the butterflies! I have collected 45 already. Most are like the ones you caught when you were home on vacations. Some are different. We are keeping them for you.

The river has good fish. If you can catch them. One day someone caught an iguana. It is like a huge lizard about five feet long including its tail. It tasted like tough chicken.

Brian and John, you would love the butterflies. We are fortunate that we have been given medicine when we were sick. The Communist soldiers have been very kind to us. I had malaria, but now I'm fine. Daddy's fine, too.

Dad and I and Auntie Betty, Uncle Norm and Aunt Joan, and the Millers and many other people are living here together. We have plenty of rice and when anyone is sick they are given sugar with their cooked rice cereal to give them extra strength. We have your last school letters written on March 2, 1975, with us. We also have the little story book that Ruthie made and sent. So I have been memorizing the Scripture verses in Brian's Bible book that he made in the Bisbee's class.

Remember that God's way is perfect. He will never leave you or forsake you. He is always with you and he has a plan for each of you, even though it is hard to understand now. He loves you very much. So do we.

Much love,

Mom and Dad

"I thought it best not to mention Norm and LuAnne's being so sick. I didn't want to worry the Johnson or Miller children."

Dick approved. "It's a fine letter, Lil. I'll just add a postscript." He took the pen and on the bottom of the letter wrote:

Psalm 91. You would be surprised to see me now with a two months' growth of beard. I want to see how you are changing and growing, too. Remember that underneath us are God's Everlasting Arms, holding us up and helping us.
God upholds us here. And each one of you.

I love you,

Dad

Deut. 33:2-7

The next day was Ho Chi Minh's birthday—another holiday respite from work. But not from the exercises they were expected to do each morning at five o'clock. Betty and Lil peeled the last of the manioc, but it was hard and not very good. They could only hope more would come.

John was really feeling low. He felt it had been the right decision for Carolyn and LuAnne to go, but now he was anxious to be reunited with them. A week after they parted he received a long letter from Carolyn.

"How are they doing?" everyone wanted to know.

"She says they had a rough time. Had a long walk at night on the last leg of the trip. Eating much better. Norm has no more fever, but is weak. He gets penicilin shots.

"Joan is staying with Carolyn and LuAnne in a separate building nearby. A kind of town hall affair. Small village.

"She says she misses me." John swallowed hard and read the rest of the letter silently.

Later that day a Jarai tribal family came to the camp and sold some dried peppers and fruit to the prisoners. The peppers added much appreciated flavor to their rice, and the fruit was a real treat. Betty was entranced by the darling baby they had with them—a ten-month-old boy, the same age as her grandchild, Rachel. Seeing the lively, fat little tribal baby made her long all the more for the dear one she had seen only one day.

Word got out that the foreign prisoners had money and would buy food from any tribespeople who came to the camp. The next day a tribal man came selling bananas. They bought two hands of the precious fruit and devoured it gratefully. They were also able to purchase red peppers, vegetables, and, once, even fresh fish.

But the most treasured treat came from a package sent by a Vietnamese wife to her POW husband. The husband willingly handed Lil a small packet of sweet candies made from powdered lotus seeds. More than the delectable confection, it was the act of sharing the missionaries appreciated.

On May 22 they were asked to fill out papers again. They complied, but didn't believe the requests for exit visas would mean anything. The paper work seemed redundant and did little to cheer them. But it was Ike's birthday and Betty was determined to make the occasion as special for the Filipino as they had made it for Dick and for Carolyn.

She spread her mosquito net over the homemade bamboo table and prepared the meal from items they had bought from the tribespeople. The forty-five-year-old guest of honor was as pleased as a child and beamed when they sang "Happy Birthday" to him. Betty was delighted to have an opportunity to make someone else happy.

She only wished she could repeat the celebration a couple of days later, for it was Gerry's seventeenth birthday. "How I would love to be with her today," Betty confided to Lil as they were taking their daily rest at the river. "Or if I could just talk with her. Assure her I'm all right."

"Let's pray for her right now," Lil suggested.

"Oh, yes," Betty sighed. "Father, you know how hard it is for me to be separated from Gerry today. I just pray You will give her a very, very special day. Comfort her heart, Lord. Give her peace . . ."

As they were returning to the house Lil mentioned, "Today is Margie Miller's birthday, too. Her thirteenth."

Betty remembered. "And I hadn't even thought about how John must be feeling. He has looked so low since Carolyn and LuAnne left, and here his first child's become a teenager and he doesn't even know where she is. At least I know Gerry is safe. We must try to encourage John."

That was no easy assignment, for they were all discouraged about their situation. They still had been given no indication how long they were going to be detained, or even what their status was. To make matters worse, they were told that night they were to sing no more Blue songs, and that included hymns.

Each day seemed to drag more than the day before. The rains kept increasing and each night felt a little colder. Lil was deeply worried because Dick appeared to grow weaker. Both Peter and Jay became ill. With Joan gone Lil was the only nurse, and she still wasn't strong herself. She kept meticulous records on each of her patients in an old account book they had in their luggage. A good deal of her time was devoted to begging medicines from the doctor.

Betty assisted as much as she could, and together they also tried to minister to the Vietnamese prisoners. With malaria spreading in the camp the order went out that they were to make new chopsticks, "proper ones," the commander said. Meaning eighteen-inch sticks with one end for serving and the other for eating.

Next they were told to boil all their clothing. Most of the

prisoners had developed scabs on their bodies from malnutrition, so they were to take steam baths by getting under their blankets or tarps with a kettle of water boiling over bamboo leaves. This remedy made them sweat, but accomplished little else.

Lil tried to convince the medical officer to give them some nivaquine, something the missionaries were used to taking, instead of treating the malaria after it developed. But she couldn't sell them on preventive medicine.

"We've got to do something," John declared. "And the only thing we can do in this situation is trust God. I've been reading in John and I came again to John 14:14, 'Yes, ask anything, using My name, and I will do it!' I think we need to claim that verse. Really test it. Pray and believe that the Lord will get us out of here within a week."

Challenged, the four missionaries bowed together and, in Jesus' name, asked God to glorify Himself by delivering them from the mosquito-ridden jungle.

Then on May 29 Betty woke achey and feverish. The news spread quickly through the longhouse: "Grandmother Mitchell" was sick. All the prisoners were concerned, for the tall missionary with her warm smile had befriended many of them. She had endeared herself by not only doing favors for them but also by allowing them to do things for her.

"I'm all right!" she protested. "I've just caught a cold."

"Betty, a cold doesn't start with a temperature of 103 plus degrees," Lil reminded. "You must start taking something."

"But I don't really feel that bad. I'll make it."

Lil called the medic anyway. He concurred with her diagnosis and put Betty on quinine and aspirin.

"I don't know how I can keep up with all the sick without her help," Lil confided to Dick and John.

"If we stay here much longer, we'll all be down," Dick predicted.

Scourge of the Tropics / 149

"And we'll all die right here in this jungle," John added.

"I keep thinking of Hank and Betty," Lil confessed. "They weren't murdered or tortured, they died of neglect and lack of medicine."

During the night Betty was stricken with chills and her temperature rose. By morning she could hardly move. She had no appetite, and just the thought of food made her vomit. She longed for a lemon. The nice sharp, bitter, clean taste of a lemon.

As she lay on her bamboo bed, her thoughts were drawn to Archie again. It was May 30. Thirteen years exactly from the day her beloved husband had been taken from her. "Thirteen years he's been gone," she remembered. "And I've not been held three months yet. Only God could keep them all this time. And only He can give us the strength to survive."

That afternoon she was given an injection, but it did nothing to relieve her discomfort. She stayed on the hard bed, her mind fading in and out—remembering the past, thinking of her family, mulling over Scriptures, trying to pray.

Another long night passed, and despite all her protests, Betty became very weak and nauseated. Whether from malaria or the quinine she didn't know, but she did consent to let Lil accompany her to the latrine. The two made quite a "Mutt-and-Jeff" appearance, with Betty a good eight inches taller than Lil. But the nurse put her arm around her friend and allowed Betty to lean on her shoulder.

They made it to the outhouse, but then Betty blacked out trying to stand up. Lil managed to get her up and struggled to get her back to the longhouse.

On another occasion they had made it just a few feet when Lil could feel Betty starting to sink. There was no way she could hold the larger woman, so she just put her arms under Betty's and let her down gradually on the wet ground.

Lil was perplexed. She didn't want to leave Betty lying

150 / Prisoners of Hope

there, but was too far from the house to call for help. Forgetting all propriety she looked over to the men's latrine and was relieved to see a Vietnamese man. She waved her arms and called to him. He glanced over, saw the problem, and came to the rescue.

With one arm around Lil's shoulder and the other around the Vietnamese Betty was half walked, half dragged back to the house. Paul spotted them coming and ran to help. Now even Betty had to admit that she was really ill.

About four o'clock in the afternoon came the welcome announcement: "You are moving. Pack up."

"Hallelujah! God answers prayer!" John shouted.

They gathered their belongings and prepared for the hike to the road. Forty-three days earlier they had stumbled through the darkness into this jungle lair; now they were incredibly weaker. Their clothes hung limply from their bodies.

They started down the trail, Betty, independently, forcing herself to walk without help. They had gone only a short distance when she vomited and fell to the ground. Determined to make it, she dragged herself up and started walking again. But after taking only a few faltering steps she fell again, this time completely unconscious.

Some of the Vietnamese prisoners came to her rescue. They fashioned a stretcher from a hammock and two sturdy bamboo poles. Dick tried to help, but the Vietnamese insisted on carrying her.

"It is our privilege to carry the grandmother," one told him.

And although it took five of the small-statured Vietnamese prisoners, who weren't strong themselves, they carried the revered American woman.

As they staggered along the four-kilometer trail, Betty's head sometimes flopped out of the stretcher and Lil would gently tuck it back in. The rest of the time Lil and Dick walked together, holding one another up. The days of captivity had taken a toll on them also, and the long, rough hike tested their endurance to the utmost.

As they neared the end, John and Ike came back to see what was taking them so long. Ike helped Dick stay vertical the last stretch of the trail.

When the POWs got Betty to the truck, they faced another obstacle. The bed of the truck was very high, and the sides of the open-topped vehicle immovable. They would have to lift the stretcher carrying Betty's limp form five feet up and then over into the truck bed. It took all their strength. Even then her body was scraped and bumped against the sides of the truck as they strained to get her in. They knew that if they didn't make it, she would be left behind. None doubted that alone in the wilderness she would die in a short time.

With a final surge of strength they heaved together and she flopped over the side and into the truck. The rest of the foreigners scrambled into the crowded truck with a dozen soldiers and all of their gear.

As the truck bounced along branches from overhanging trees raked across the prisoners. Lil tenderly bent over Betty to protect her face. Betty had been given no medicine because the medic was afraid the reaction of the quinine added to a bouncy trip would cause her to vomit too much. With nothing more she could do for her patient, Lil fanned her, trying to keep her as cool as possible as the truck rumbled on toward an unknown destination.

Family members still await the return of husband and father Archie Mitchell. (Top) Betty Mitchell and children one year after Archie's capture. (Bottom left) Betty Mitchell with son Glenn and daughter Geraldine, holding "Silly" the monkey, in Banmethuot in 1971. (Bottom right) Betty Mitchell, her children, and friend Delmer Scott on Christmas Day 1965 in Banmethuot.

9

"Fat City"

Although the back of the truck was not crowded, it was a nightmarish ride. The sun was beastly hot, the road—they guessed it was one of the many branches of the Ho Chi Minh Trail—narrow and uneven.

All were pondering their uncertain future. Where were they being taken this time? And would they be reunited with the sick who had been sent ahead to the field hospital?

The dilemma of the unknown was hardest for John. Out there somewhere in the foreboding jungle were Carolyn and LuAnne. Would he see them soon? He fervently hoped so. It had been bad enough not knowing if his oldest three were safe, now to be apart from Carolyn and LuAnne seemed almost too much.

The air turned cooler and by nightfall a cold drizzle had begun. The truck pulled to a stop at a deserted tribal village.

In the semidarkness they could make out a group of houses

encircled by a stockade fence. Probably a Jarai village turned into a prison camp, Dick opined.

John heard a familiar voice and ran. "Carolyn!" He smothered her in his arms, overjoyed at being together again. LuAnne was sleeping peacefully just inside a house, but he couldn't wait. He pulled the sleeping child onto his lap and kissed her soundly.

"Daddy!" came the childish squeal, and two little arms grasped his neck so tightly he choked, but he didn't care.

"Yes, Sweetheart. Daddy's got his girls back. Praise the Lord!"

He remembered Betty and, with Carolyn following, hurried back to the truck. He and the other men helped her out and raised her to where she could hold on to his and Paul's shoulders. They took her into a house and eased her onto a bamboo bed.

The others joined in the reunion, exclaiming their joy at just being together again.

"You all look so much better," Lil smiled at Joan.

Joan could only say, "But you look so thin," as she gazed at the scrawny, emaciated looking newcomers. It was unbelievable how they had deteriorated during the past two weeks at Camp Wilderness.

Betty was obviously worst off. "She's been very nauseated," Lil reported. "Can't keep anything down and is probably dehydrated. She did say she would love the taste of a lemon. You wouldn't happen to have any here, would you?"

"Would you believe?" Joan grinned. "I'll make her some lemonade."

While all the backslapping and hugging had been going on, a dark-skinned, oriental looking man had stood back shyly watching.

"Oh, this is Bog," LuAnne announced, leading the stranger over to the group. "He is King Number Two. My Daddy is

"Fat City" / 155

King Number One, but Bog is Number Two, 'cause he's my friend."

"Well, looks as if you've captured my daughter's affection," John smiled, holding out his hand.

Bog's understanding of English wasn't quite up to John's vocabulary, but he got the idea and gave a hardy handshake. "I like kids," he said, "I got eight boys. Home, in Philippines.

"My name Arellano Bugarin is hard to say, so everyone call me Bog, like LuAnne says."

Dick had investigated their new "home" and was pleased to note it had a couple of distinct advantages. It was smaller, so just their group would be living there, and there were four small rooms partitioned off by woven bamboo walls. They would never keep out sounds, but this was the closest to a little privacy the couples had had since they were captured. It was decided that one room would be assigned to Betty and the other rooms to the three couples. LuAnne shared her parents' room and the single men shared the front section of the house.

They discovered that in this camp they would be expected to do their own cooking. "But they also said we would be allowed to go to market and spend our own money on any extras we wanted," Carolyn explained.

"How far would that be?" Paul asked.

"About six kilometers, I think," she replied.

After eating the rice crunchies and rice coffee that had been prepared for them, they sat around and talked, filling each other in on what had happened while they were separated.

"Did you have commodious accommodations in the hospital?" Peter asked.

"Well, it wasn't really a hospital," Norm explained. "I stayed in a cement building with holes where artillery shots had hit the building. Very dirty, not well kept at all. A two-room school, but the second room had been destroyed by shelling. I slept on two long school desks pushed together.

"The most impressive thing about the place was the flies. You wouldn't believe them. They were so big that one day they pushed over the outhouse!"

The laughter this comment brought encouraged the exuberant Canadian to continue the description.

"Honest, those were the biggest flies you ever saw in your life. As big as my thumb! I just couldn't believe God made flies like that. I think they must be the result of atomic fallout or something."

The explosion of laughter that followed was mixed with a few tears. "Oh, Norm, it's so good to hear you joking again," Lil said, wiping the corners of her eyes. "You were so sick when you left I really wasn't sure you'd make it. We have so much to be thankful for."

"Yes," John agreed emphatically. Turning to Carolyn, he explained, "You see, Honey, we had a prayer meeting the other night and decided to claim John 14:14, about whatever we asked in Jesus' name would be granted, and we asked to be taken out of there before the end of the month. And here we are! Now we need to thank Him for answered prayer."

The next morning, the first day of June, Betty had a ringing in her ears and a very heavy head, but no fever. She found it difficult to hear the worship services that were led that Sunday morning by Lil, but what she could hear lifted her spirits. It was her twenty-eighth wedding anniversary, and she sorely needed a lift.

Still extremely weak, she was able to fill in the past two days in her diary and then noted her anniversary: *"I'm more lonesome than ever for Archie since I've been here. I keep thinking that if they bring all POWs here, he will be coming."*

She lay on her hard, bamboo bed reminiscing about the days leading up to their wedding. Strangely, it had been tragedy and sorrow that first brought them together. A mysterious balloon bomb, floated across the Pacific by the Japanese during World

War II, had exploded during a Sunday school picnic, killing Archie's first wife, Elsie, and Betty's youngest brother and sister.

After the funerals many thought the young pastor should go on to a different church, away from the constant reminders in Bly, Oregon. But Archie felt he was needed in the little logging town. Besides Betty's family, three others had lost sons in that blast. Archie considered it his responsibility to help them in the hour of common grief.

Often as he visited Betty's home the Patzke family gathered around and talked about their loss. This sharing of sorrow was a time of healing for them. All the families drew close together; indeed, the experience drew the entire church closer.

Betty had already had a year of study at Simpson Bible College and that summer between sessions she joined in the activities of the small church the Lord had used to bring her family to Christ. She and Archie were just naturally drawn together.

She was planning on going to the mission field as a single woman after finishing her next year at Simpson. The Lord had used the death of her little sister, who was a mission volunteer, to lead her to this commitment. Then, late in the summer just before returning to school, she attended a church camp.

Betty smiled to herself as she remembered that Saturday night at camp. They had a testimonial meeting around a campfire. She had her hair done up in pin curls with a scarf around it so it would look nice for church services in the morning. She had no inkling this was to be one of the most fateful nights of her life.

After the meeting broke up Archie suggested they go for a walk. They had gone on walks together before, so she thought nothing special about it. But as they strolled along, he took her hand for the first time.

As they got farther from the group to a place where they

were alone, he stopped, took her other hand, turning her toward him. "Betty, I love you," he told her simply. She remembered thinking, "How can he say that, when I have my hair up in curlers?" But as she pictured the precious scene in her mind, she knew Archie loved her for herself, not for the way she looked.

During the time of separation after her return to school they wrote long, personal, loving letters. Making plans for the future when they could serve the Lord together overseas.

They announced their engagement the next Easter, but by this time no one was surprised to find the young pastor had found just the right partner to share his future. It had become evident to their friends and relatives that the two shared a strong bond of love and friendship.

On June 1, 1947, they were married in the little church where everyone knew and loved them. Betty wore a long, white, handmade dress for the candlelight ceremony that followed the evening service.

Betty had always felt sad that only one of the pictures came out—the one with her cutting the cake at the reception held afterward at the Patzke home.

That June 1 seemed a long time ago. Betty thought of the many anniversaries they had enjoyed together. So many good times. She and Archie had always shared laughter. People frequently remarked what a good team they made, how well they worked together. Perhaps it was because any task she shared with Archie had seemed more an opportunity for service than work.

And then, unbidden, came remembrance of that first wedding anniversary after Archie was taken captive—their fifteenth—and she expected him to be released, to come walking out of the jungle to celebrate with her and the children. But the day ended and she was alone. Alone for many anniversaries now.

She remembered the twentieth, too, for that was the day Becki had graduated from high school. She recalled sitting at the Dalat School that bright, sunny day and watching their daughter give the salutatory address. Becki was becoming such a fine young lady. Betty had thought over and over, "How very proud Archie would be of her today."

That day her four children were with her. How could she have taken the sorrow without them? People were always telling her how brave she was, but only the Lord knew how hard it was to be without Archie on days like that. She knew from experience the truth of the Scripture, "My strength is made perfect in weakness."

And now here she was. In captivity, and so very sick. Separated not only from her husband, but from all her children as well. One hope sustained her. Archie might be near. He might come to this very camp. Walk through that door. Each time someone entered the house she looked up, hoping to see her husband return to her as an anniversary present from the Lord.

But he didn't come.

Just when Betty was feeling so alone, Lil came bringing more lemonade. "Thank you, Lord, for Lil," Betty prayed. "For all my dear friends. For bringing us out of the jungle. For answered prayer. For not leaving me alone today."

And that still, small Voice that had become familiar to her over the years whispered, "I will never leave you, nor forsake you. Cast your burdens on Me and I will give you peace."

All that came that day was rain. A cold, chilling, continuous drizzle that made the trip to the river for water a slippery, precarious adventure for the men.

"It's a long, slimy trip down there and back," Norm told the recent arrivals, "but we're expected to get our own water here and to do our own boiling."

"Maybe we could catch some rainwater," Paul suggested. "Might save a few trips." So they put out some cans, but it wasn't raining hard enough to get much.

That night it cleared off some, but was cold. After having spent forty-three nights in the middle of the jungle it was a pleasure to see the starry heavens. There were few trees in this camp, and the numerous plants, sweet potatoes, and peppers were low growers that didn't block the view of the skies.

With help Betty was able to go outside to see God's magnificent handiwork. "It's so beautiful," she exclaimed. "It shows God's orderliness. He has a plan for everything, doesn't He?"

She was thankful that His plan for her included women companions at this time. Carolyn helped as much as she could, but LuAnne demanded most of her attention. Joan and Lil were almost always at Betty's bedside, applying their nursing skills. With their assistance Betty valiantly tried to maintain her equilibrium on the slippery path to the outhouse. After falling in the mud once, she was more willing to accept their support.

"What would I do without them?" she murmured when safely back in bed. She thought of Dr. Ardel Vietti being held so many years with only men. And Betty Olsen who had died without the gentle, comforting administrations of another woman. Even in the darkest of circumstances Betty found reason to praise the Lord.

Paul returned from the first market trip all aglow with a travelogue of the village. After nearly three months of prison life it had been good just to enjoy the sights and smells of living as the people moved about in freedom. They were promised a market trip every ten days. With escorts, of course.

"We're going to have to come to some kind of decision about what to buy on these trips," Paul declared. "Some of us were taken with no money at all, and others had quite a bit of cash with them. It doesn't seem fair not to give an even shake to those without funds."

"Well, I had gone to the bank and gotten our monthly allotment just before we were captured, since we had planned on going to Nhatrang to be with our kids, so we have quite a bit," John said frankly. "But I vote for pooling all our resources and dividing evenly."

"I'll second that," Norm agreed, "since we have some cash to throw in the kitty."

Everyone was enthusiastic about sharing, and those who had little or nothing to give were not made to feel beholden. "We're all in this together," Dick commented, expressing the feelings of the entire group.

Because the climate was a good deal cooler than in the jungle the prisoners were issued longjohns, jackets, and extra shirts. The used South Vietnamese army jackets still bore the names and numbers of the original recipients. They could only guess what had happened to the previous owners.

After fourteen days of medicine supplemented by fresh fruits and vegetables from the market, Betty was looking better. As soon as she was ambulatory she insisted on helping with the chores. One of these was picking leaves so they might have greens in their diet.

One day a guard came up to the women and demanded, "Why are you picking those leaves?"

"What did you say?" Betty asked, in her halting Vietnamese.

"Why—do—you—pick—leaves?" the guard repeated slowly.

"You want some leaves?" Betty asked.

"No, that's not what I said," the *bo doi* shouted. "You do not have permission to pick those leaves. You must stop now!"

"I'm sorry, you are speaking too fast. I can't understand."

"Stop picking!" he yelled. Of course, all the time Betty was having this discourse with the guard, Joan and Carolyn were picking as fast as they could.

"Oh," Betty replied innocently, "you don't want us to pick leaves?"

"That is correct. Tell your friends to stop now."

"Of course. We wouldn't want to be uncooperative. We obey all camp rules." She walked over to the other two and said, "We'd better not take any more."

"That's okay," Joan replied. "We have enough for a couple more meals."

Betty continued to improve, though she still had a hard time keeping her food down. She enjoyed drinking hot milk and nibbling on roasted peanuts, but her weight continued to drop. They had prayer, asking for the Lord's healing strength, and gradually she got better.

But LuAnne had a recurrence of tonsilitis and ran a high temperature. As the fever hung on day after day the Millers became worried. When Carolyn begged the camp doctor for medicine he seemed sincerely concerned, but told her gently, "I'm sorry. I just don't have what she needs. There is nothing here I can give her."

The distraught mother returned to their partitioned cubbyhole in the house. John, sitting beside his sleeping child, looked up expectantly.

"It's no use," Carolyn sighed. "There just isn't any medicine for her. I believe if the doctor had any, he would have given it to me."

"I don't know how much longer she can last like this," John replied, looking at the beloved child who seemed to be wasting away before their eyes. "Her throat is so sore she can't eat anything. If the infection doesn't kill her, she'll starve."

"There's nothing we can do, John, except commit her to the Lord. We know He loves LuAnne and knows what is best for her. Perhaps it would be the most merciful thing for Him to take her now."

"That's true. If we are all going to die in captivity, it would be best for her to go first. I don't know how she would take it if one or both of us should die. With such an uncertain future, what more can we do than accept what He deems best for her?"

The two knelt by their cherished daughter and prayed, committing her to God's goodness and love, believing that He would do whatever was in her best interest. Even if it meant taking her to Himself. They finished praying, then lay back silently on their bamboo bed.

Shortly there came a rustling at the door. Carolyn opened it to a stranger. "Here, here is some medicine for the little girl," he said, extending a small package.

"Did the doctor send this?" she asked. "What are the instructions for giving it?"

"I don't know. You will have to ask him," he replied quietly and turned and walked off.

"Thank you," Carolyn called after him, a little perplexed that the doctor would send medicine and not instructions. When it was time for sick call Carolyn returned to the doctor with the medicine for instructions.

"I didn't send any medicine," the medic said, puzzled. "I don't have any to send. Let me see what you have." As he opened the packet his eyes rounded with wonder. "Why, this is exactly what she needs!" he exclaimed. "Give it to her."

Hurrying back with the instructions for dosage, Carolyn started LuAnne on the medicine immediately. That same day her fever broke and by the next day she was feeling fine.

The stranger who had delivered the medicine was never seen again. But they had no doubt that God had sent him. It seemed the longer they were in captivity the more gracious the Lord became in answering prayer.

Lil was next to be hit with chills, vomiting, and fever of malaria. The frail nurse who had given of herself so unselfishly was now bedridden. She was still very sick when the group was visited by Spectacles the first time since they had moved to this camp.

"You are all filling out your reports as requested. This is good, but do not omit anything for your words will be checked. We want you to eat more. You are becoming too thin. Keep happy and keep healthy," he instructed them.

The political officer and another "friend" from the North stayed with the prisoners for about a half hour, but gave no hint of what was to become of them. As always Betty asked if he had found any information about Archie, and the reply was negative.

The next day they were given three kilos of fresh beef. They were ecstatic. They cooked about a third for supper that evening and hung the rest from the rafters, out of reach of the rats. They were also issued lots of vitamins. Obviously, Spectacles wanted them fattened up for some reason.

They sat around the campfire watching the stars that night and speculated about the improved treatment. "Wonder what they have in mind?" Norm, ever the optimist, asked the others.

"Who knows," Jay grunted.

"Next week is the end of school in Dalat," Betty noted. "It would really be wonderful if we could be released before our children are scattered."

"If not, I presume the children will be sent to the guardians assigned to them in our wills," Dick mused.

"I'd rather have them in Asia," Joan stressed. "At least in the same part of the world with us. It would really be hard for my folks to keep them in their small apartment. Besides, that would make our separation seem permanent."

"Yeah," Norm agreed, "I wonder just what we'll find when we are released. What has happened in the world that we haven't heard about."

"What about our own families?" Lil pondered. "My parents are in their eighties and I can't help wondering what our captivity has done to their health."

"One thing about this experience though, it makes you get your perspectives straight," Norm contended. "I mean what good does an education or money or any of the status symbols of civilization mean here? Nothing. When everything has been stripped from you, you realize the one thing that endures, that they can never take from you, is your faith. That verse in Romans 8, you know, 'Neither death, nor life, nor angels, and so on, can separate us from the love of God,' means much more to me now than it ever did."

"And that faith has to help us not only trust Him to care for us, but also that He will be with our loved ones," Betty added.

On June 20 the group marked their hundredth day in captivity. It was three weeks since they had moved to the new camp they now called "Fat City" because of the market trips that allowed them to eat better. Betty celebrated the occasion by taking her first faltering trip to the river. She finally had the strength to walk down so she could bathe and wash her clothes and hair. To feel refreshed made the long trip there and back worth the effort.

The next day she made the trip again and was delighted to catch a butterfly which she hoped would encourage Lil, who continued very ill. Norm and Paul were sick also. It seemed all of them were never well at the same time. The cold, damp weather might have had something to do with it. They were sleeping with their jackets on.

Visitors kept popping in. As usual they said, "Keep your health up! Exercise! Keep happy!" But the officers were not happy when the foreign POWs asked about rumors they had been hearing from some of the wives of Vietnamese prisoners who were allowed in camp from time to time.

"They say the South is not all that peaceful and happy as we have been led to believe," Paul said. "We heard that there was a demonstration by the wives of some of the POWs and two were killed. That their irons were taken from them, and all radios confiscated. That the only news they are allowed to hear is from the loudspeakers that broadcast Radio Hanoi."

"There have been some problems," one of the officers admitted. "But you must realize that the South fell much quicker than even we had anticipated. Even in the wake of a glorious victory such as ours there are adjustments to be made. Be assured that the reunified Vietnam will be peaceful."

After the officer left the foreigners heard that he was a two-star general.

"I wonder why they are bringing in the big brass?" Paul asked rhetorically.

Later they learned that all POWs holding the rank of lieutenant were to be released. It was nice to know some were being freed, but not so comforting to realize that they as foreigners held higher status in the camp.

On June 26 Lil developed a high fever and Betty sponged her to bring down the temperature. While Betty gently rubbed and squeezed, she began reminiscing about Becki's wedding, for it was the fourth anniversary of that occasion. "I really wanted to go," Betty said. "Especially since Dave's parents were dead, it seemed that at least I should be there. Our Vietnam branch had agreed that I should go and New York headquarters granted permission. But, of course, it would be at my own expense and I didn't have money for the flight.

"Then just a few days later I got a letter from Becki and it said, 'Sit down when you read this letter.' So I sat down and read that some dear friends wanted to give Dave and Becki a wedding present, and the present was a ticket for me to come to their wedding. Good thing I was sitting down!

"I went early so I could be at Becki's graduation from nurses' training. And Loretta was already in the States at school. The

International Church in Saigon and the Vietnam missionaries took up an offering to send Glenn and Gerry home—a complete surprise to them. So all our family were there, and forty-nine Dalat School kids. Grady Mangham performed the ceremony—it was so beautiful!

"Glenn gave his sister away. But really I didn't feel I was losing a daughter, for David became a part of our family instead. And that's such a comfort to me. David is strong and dependable, very much like his father was. It's good to know Glenn and Loretta are with them in San Diego.

"You knew that Becki and Dave had been assigned as medical missionaries to Cambodia. I wonder now where they will go. I'm so happy they love the Lord and will be serving Him some place."

Lil smiled and whispered, "I'm glad for you." Lil was weak and looked terribly pitiful with the eye infection she had developed. And to add to her discomfort she had developed a huge boil on her back. Betty longed to do something to relieve the dear friend who had nursed her so lovingly.

Later in the day the medic came and said Lil must go to the hospital in the morning. "Can Dick come with me?" she pleaded. "Please. I don't want to go without Dick."

"I can't promise. I'll ask," was all the doctor would say.

"Oh, pray," Lil begged her friends. "Please pray that Dick can come with me. I don't want to d—to go alone."

It was hard for Betty to contemplate being separated from Lil. If there were only some way she could repay her for the loving care lavished while she was ill. Would they ever see each other again in this life? she wondered.

"It's for Lil's benefit," she kept telling herself. "She could die without proper medical attention. Just let Dick go with her," she continued, her thoughts turning into prayer. "Please, please, dear Jesus. Don't make Lil go through the agony of being separated from her husband."

All of the missionaries felt the same burden and throughout the night prayer was lifted that the Phillipses might not be separated.

The next morning the guards came for Lil with a stretcher. And with permission for Dick to accompany her.

"All of this is in His hands," Betty comforted, as the slight figure was placed on the stretcher. "He has a purpose in it all. We'll be praying for you, Lil."

Dick was too weak himself to carry any baggage, so some of the Vietnamese POWs went along with them to take their belongings. It was all he could do to walk the distance, but his desire to stay with his wife enabled him to endure.

"The Lord be with you," Betty called after them in benediction.

(Opposite page) Special occasions are highlights for Betty Mitchell and her children. (Top left) Betty Mitchell and her children at Becki's high school graduation in 1967. The day also commemorated Archie and Betty's twentieth wedding anniversary. (Top right) Glenn, Loretta, Gerry, and Betty Mitchell at Loretta's graduation in 1970. (Bottom left) Betty Mitchell, proud mom, with nurse daughter, Becki, in 1971. (Bottom right) Becki Mitchell and David Thompson, children of tragedy but a happy bride and groom. David's parents were killed at Banmethuot in 1968. Becki's father was captured in 1962 and her mother in 1975. David, an M.D., and Becki, an R.N., are assigned as medical missionaries to Gabon, Africa.

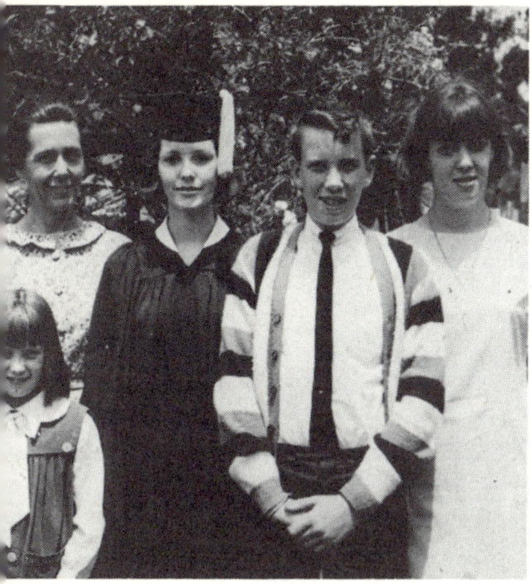
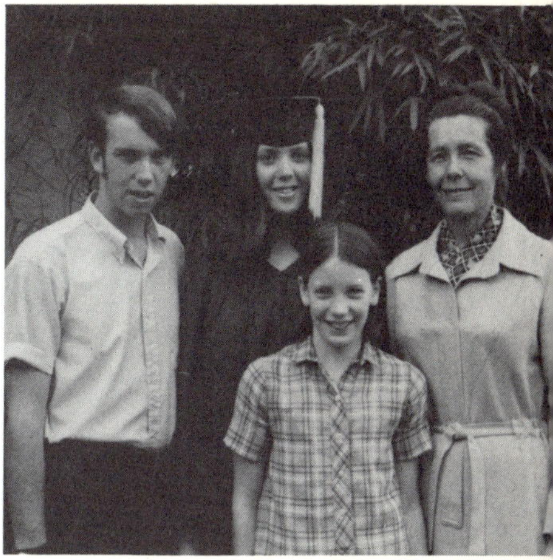
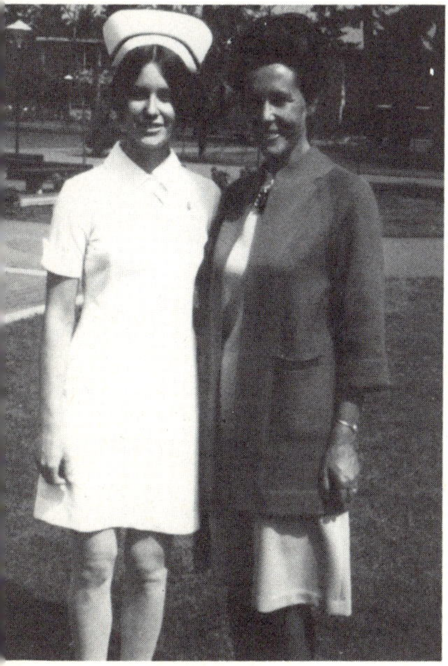
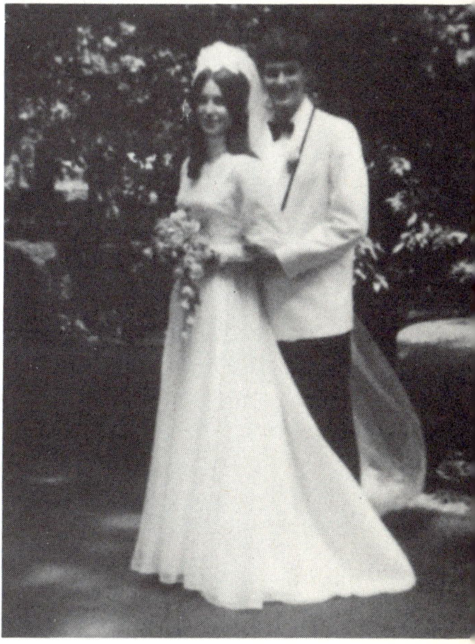

10

Together Again

With Dick and Lil gone five missionaries, LuAnne, two Filipinos (Ike and Bog), a USAID officer (Paul), an American student (Jay), and an Australian broadcaster (Peter) constituted the foreign population left in Fat City to battle with weather, colds, sickness, and an ever increasing number of termites.

The fight with the insects had begun when the pests had tried to capture the Millers' quarters. Pulling out infested thatch and replacing with new had merely provoked a change in strategy. New battlefronts emerged. First in the front of the house, and then one miserable night Betty found her bed crawling with thousands of the insects.

The men came and doused her quarters four times with water and the bugs retreated. At least Betty hoped they had, for she had no other place to sleep and spunkily climbed back into bed and went to sleep.

The prisoners won that battle, but lost the war. On Jay's birthday, July 6, they abandoned the building to the victors and moved into a new house that had been built for them in the potato patch.

Until they started carrying their belongings to new quarters the prisoners hadn't realized they had become great junk collectors. They had shovels, hoes, pick heads, pieces of hose, wire, machetes, anything and everything that seemed useful. They had such an assortment of equipment that often the NVA came to borrow from their inventory.

While all this was being transported to their new dwelling Paul noticed something that brought a cheer from the men. A well!

"Boy, this is great!" Norm exclaimed. "Terrific!" And he started to draw some water.

The well wasn't in very good condition, the handle was flimsy, but it sure beat a slippery trip down to the river and a long struggle back with loaded cans.

The new house lacked a clothesline, so Norm wandered out to the barbed wire fence and began unwinding the wire from the posts. When he had enough he rolled it up and took it home. It worked fine.

Another time he spotted a big strand of wire on the ground. The NVA were getting ready for a big camp meeting and the wire was being used to install some loudspeakers for the occasion. As he strolled by, Norm casually scooped up the wire and put it under his jacket. This was braided into a much needed belt for Peter.

The wire proved to be a very practical item and when they wanted more to tie up bundles Norm went out with a machete. While Joan talked to the guard, he hacked away at the wires until he had what they needed. Placing it under his coat, he and Joan returned to the house.

While Norm was playing "Hogan's Heroes," their captors were having a "revival" Communist style. Or so Peter termed the series of evening meetings that had started in a bamboo arbor nearby.

"Yeah," Paul grinned, "and they've brought in a 'Billy Graham' to deliver the message," referring to the main speaker, a general.

The two laughed, enjoying what they thought were digs at the missionaries. To their surprise, the missionaries agreed.

"*Revival* is the right word," Carolyn concurred. "They sing songs to the glory of their revolution, read from a book, listen to an inspirational message, then call for listeners to 'repent' of their sins."

"Right," John continued her line, "and they 'rededicate' themselves to the goals of their revolution."

"And give testimonies about how Communism has changed their lives," Joan added.

"All they need is an offertory," Norm quipped.

"But they are sincere," Carolyn noted seriously. "They really believe that Communism is the answer to all the world's problems, and they are willing to dedicate their very lives to further its spread."

"It's just a shame that Christians don't always have that same dedication," Betty mused.

"Oh, I wouldn't worry if I were you," Peter sneered. "You're just as fanatical as any Communist I've ever come across."

"Thank you, Peter. I consider that a real compliment," Betty replied.

"But at least the Communists are practical," Jay put in. "They're concerned with helping people in the here and now, not in the sweet by and by. And they're egalitarian."

"Aw, now, Jay," Paul disagreed, "they have a caste system, too. The political officers are the priests; they walk around in pointy-toed, storebought shoes and nice trim tailored uniforms. They each have their own little black bag and a transistor radio. While the grunts wear rubber sandals, pith helmets, and the same uniforms for five years."

"Don't forget, Christians are interested in practical things, too," John interjected. "Missionaries do lots of humanitarian work."

"Yeah, and change the people's culture in doing it," Paul countered.

Carolyn reacted strongly, "We don't change their cultures. Certainly not the good parts."

Paul couldn't let this pass. "Carolyn, you forget that I'm a member of a Raday family. I've lived with these people long enough to know. And you have changed things among the Bru. Why, one time I tried to get some of the Bru to do a buffalo sacrifice dance and none of them knew it. I finally found a couple of old men who wiggled around when I paid them enough. But it was obvious they didn't really know it either."

"Just one problem with that, Paul," Carolyn smiled. "The Raday dance at a buffalo sacrifice, but the Bru do not. At a funeral, maybe, but never for the buffalo. You are the one guilty of changing custom by paying them to do something that is not in their culture!"

"I think it's about time to turn in," John advised, sensing that the verbal duel was heating up.

"Yeah, you're right," Carolyn conceded reluctantly.

Since they wanted to present a united front to the Communists, the whole group had worked at getting along, but opposite viewpoints sometimes made it hard. Especially when statements were passed degrading the work to which the missionaries had dedicated their lives.

The next morning when the men went to get water from the well, the handle broke off. The camp cook came storming over. "You can't use that. You can't use this well anymore. Go to the river."

"Why can't we use it?" the men demanded. "We don't want to go all the way down to the river all the time."

"I say you can't use it," the cook yelled back.

"Well, we'll see about that," Norm snorted. And he and John marched over to the camp commander. After they presented their views the CO went to talk to the cook. The prisoners held back as the two got into a fight over the well. Finally the officer shouted, "I have said it!"

The dispute was settled.

To the prisoners he said, "You can use the well twice a day. Four cans of water each time. Morning and afternoon. If that is not enough, go to the river."

"Well, we won that battle," Norm announced proudly to the women.

"Yeah, but if you don't learn to shut up sometimes, you are going to win a battle and lose your life," Joan warned. "You really scare me when you confront them like that. You need to remember they hold our lives in their hands."

"But we just can't kowtow all the time," Norm shot back. "If we hadn't spoken up or showed any boldness, we wouldn't have gotten to use the well. And you do the same thing when you argue over medicine."

Norm was not so confident a couple of days later when he dashed into the house with his pupils dilated, breathing hard, and a thin coating of sweat on his brow. "I almost got killed," he panted to his wife.

"What happened?"

"Well, I was going down to the river when this guard lit into me. Real belligerent like. I don't know what was wrong with him."

"He had just had a fight with Jay, that's what was wrong," Joan explained.

"Well, I didn't know that. So he yelled at me, 'Where are you going?' And I said, 'To the river,' and started walking.

"Then I heard the click of the safety on his rifle. I thought, 'He's bluffing, he won't shoot me in the back.' But I wasn't sure. But I figured, 'Well, if I'm going to die, I'm going to die. But I'm not going to be a coward.' And I kept on walking."

"Oh, Norm, you'll give me heart failure. I'd rather be married to a live coward than to a dead fool."

"Well, I guess that was pretty dumb. I didn't know he'd had a run-in with Jay. I guess I'm just fed up with this whole situation."

Norm wasn't the only one who was losing patience as one monotonous day followed another. They could get no information as to their status, on how long they were going to be kept prisoners, or if they would ever be released.

Two weeks after the Phillipses had left Dick was brought back one day for interrogation. He reported that Lil's eye was much better and the carbuncle on her back had been surgically removed. "She's still having a lot of pain though," he added sadly, "and seems to be developing more and more carbuncles."

The number of sick POWs at Fat City was increasing every day. Jay came down with malaria. Carolyn developed a severely infected ulcer on her right thigh. Although there weren't as many mosquitoes here as in Wilderness, those in residence were powerful.

Besides suffering from fevers and infections, the gaunt, scraggly foreigners were steadily losing hair, a sure sign of malnutrition in spite of the added variety in their diet. They were concerned about this, especially Bog who spent hours peering into a hand mirror, inspecting his scalp.

Their captors noticed and were alarmed to the point of ordering extra rations for the non-Asians on grounds they were bigger and needed more food. Part of the extra was one can of

Spam-like meat. Although they dubbed it "dog meat," it was nutritious. This and other additional food was divided equally with the Filipinos.

They were also promised new clothes. Shirts for the men and material for the women. Whenever their treatment improved the prisoners speculated if their captors might not be preparing them for release. Despite previous disappointments, their hopes rose again.

Carolyn spent much of her time putting hot packs on her ulcerated leg, trying to draw out the painful infection. She was thankful that LuAnne had Bog's attention. The Filipino had developed a strong attachment to the blue-eyed charmer and played for hours at anything LuAnne's creative imagination invented. Often she was the princess and he the slave, or the dog or cat or whatever she wanted him to be.

After being in a world of adults for four months it seemed almost natural that she would invent a playmate her age. "Lurleen" became a regular participant in the games LuAnne and Bog played. "Lurleen" ate with LuAnne, slept with her, and sometimes even argued with her.

Jay's temperature soared, and two POWs came and carried him away to the hospital. Their ranks were dwindling. A week later they got a letter from Jay, saying he was feeling much better. Lil had added a note. She was still extremely ill and had developed two more carbuncles, but was receiving better food.

Norm's birthday came a couple of days later, on July 22. His day wasn't very cheerful for he was feeling poorly again. Joan wasn't sure if it was a repeat of malaria or just depression after having his hopes up a few days before. He didn't want a celebration; all he wanted was to see his kids.

All of them were feeling down. The few bright spots in the next weeks for Betty were the occasional letters from Lil and the times she and Joan spent together at the river. The two had become very close during the past year, first in Banmethuot and now in captivity. Joan found Betty to be a very open, warm, understanding person. One with whom she could pray comfortably.

The missionaries had concluded a study of Colossians together. They had shared their feelings about Philippians 1:29. As one Sunday John spoke on the difficulties David had faced, they identified with these. Perhaps more than any other book, the Psalms brought them the greatest comfort.

Many times as Betty was reminded of her promise not to murmur or complain, she was grateful that they were permitted to have the comfort of God's Word. What a privilege!

No longer in the jungle, they could now enjoy counting stars. On clear nights they lay on benches outdoors, eyes scanning the heavens. Paul taught them how to spot satellites by catching them in the periphery of vision. They divided into teams: one team counted shooting stars, the other satellites. The record score for one evening was thirteen shooting stars to six satellites.

The camp commander at Fat City was very big on exercise, so the men rigged up a bamboo bar and each morning did a few chinups. Paul got them started jogging, but that didn't last long. The guards got nervous at the sight of the foreigners running around camp. They looked too free.

The emphasis on exercise did provide a little humor, for the guards were supposed to exercise, too. Each morning they were to divide into groups and start calling off numbers: *"Mot, hai, ba, BON."* Religiously, each day the singsong chanting began, but when the prisoners looked out the window they saw no one in the yard. The guards would still be in bed calling out the words.

Toward the end of the exercise period they would struggle out and stand around with their hands in their pockets, the leader calling, *"Mot, hai, ba, BON,"* and the rest obediently echoing the chant.

Much more of the time was spent just living. Carrying water, boiling it, cooking, cleaning, existing.

To battle boredom and sharpen appetites the women experimented with new recipes. By boiling the strong salty taste out of salt pork, they came up with a delicious sweet and sour concoction. Another favorite was pseudo fish sticks made from dried fish powder. But the big hit was Ike's "doughnuts."

The first time he made them surreptitiously by grinding wet rice into flour and adding milk powder and sugar. After dunking for ten or fifteen minutes, the pastries still retained their toughness. But they were tasty and everyone enjoyed them.

When the women added shortening to the next batch they came out softer. After that making doughnuts became a group affair. With Ike and the women supervising, the men took turns pounding the rice into flour. Then LuAnne helped Betty shape the treats.

The one big disagreement that arose during this period was over spending money on liquor. The drinkers said they should have the freedom to spend their share of the money any way they wanted; the others thought it a needless waste.

"We don't know how long our money will have to last," Betty reasoned. "We should spend it wisely on things that are good for our bodies."

The dispute remained a bone of contention.

At the end of July the Millers celebrated their anniversaries.

"Anniversar*ies,* plural?" Peter asked.

"Yes, we were married in Saigon, you see," John explained. "We had the civil ceremony one day and the church ceremony the next. So we actually have two." As a present to his beloved, John carved some little wooden spoons and a salad fork and spoon set from *k'te* wood.

July ended with one plus. Jay came walking home from the hospital, looking good and reporting Lil had improved.

On Friday, August 1, Betty made a special entry in her diary: *Rachel Joy, one year old. How well I remember last year. May the hand of God be upon her each day of her life. And give her parents wisdom to raise her. Happy birthday, my dear granddaughter. My prayers are with you and all my family. I think of you today.*

It was also Nate Miller's birthday, his eighth. "You really do miss them in a different way on special days, don't you," Carolyn admitted. "I've been thinking about Nate all day, wondering where he is, how he is celebrating his day, what kind of cake he had. That kind of thing. And then remembering when he was born in Danang. And the first time we left him at school."

"I remember that," John joined in. "He was at the gate, and asked, 'How come you say you love me and you are leaving me here?' And we said it was because we loved him that we were leaving him. It seemed to satisfy him.

"Then when we went back to visit and asked him how everything was, he said, 'Oh, fine,'" Carolyn continued. "And he was all happy and smiling. Because the school was a happy place. I just hope he's in a happy place today."

Peter and Paul returned from market earlier than expected. "Communism will never work," Paul laughed. "The good ol' free enterprise system is just natural to all mankind."

"What do you mean?" Betty asked.

"Well, each time we go to market we have a shorter trip. The tribespeople aren't dumb. They catch on to what we like and keep setting up store closer and closer to the camp," he explained, setting down the bananas, peanuts, candles, and coffee they had purchased.

"Also on the way out the political officer gave us a very interesting piece of advice," Paul informed them with a grin.

"What's that?" the ever curious Canadian asked.

"Said we should spend as much money as we could. Now, just why do you think they would want us to use up our South

Vietnamese currency?"

"Hey, that does sound like something may be brewing," John joined in.

The group gathered around, all chattering at once. This was really a hopeful bit of news. They concluded they would be either released or taken to North Vietnam.

"That would be something!" Jay exclaimed. "I would really love to see Hanoi."

"I'd rather see the Golden Gate at San Francisco," Carolyn said decisively. "A trip to Hanoi might seem like a big adventure to you, but I want to be with my kids."

"Well, it's just that not many Americans have been to Hanoi," Jay defended himself.

"Betty, you were assigned there, weren't you?" Joan asked.

"No, we were there for language study when we first came to the field, then we were assigned to Sontay, which isn't far from there, but I never got there. Archie visited there only once."

The anticipation that something was going to happen had bolstered everyone's flagging spirits. "Now if Dick and Lil would rejoin us, I'd feel better about it," Betty commented. "They've been gone over a month. It just doesn't seem right for our group to be split up, and I would certainly hate to leave here without them."

On the ninth of August they missed the Phillipses even more, for it was little Johnny Phillips' seventh birthday. "I know how lonely they must feel for him today," Carolyn sympathized.

"Yes," Betty said, "Lil is such a devoted mother, I know it's hard for her to be separated from her 'Bunker Baby,' as she calls him."

"Why's that?" Joan asked.

"Because she spent three days in a bunker during Tet of '68, before he was born."

"You can tell how much she misses her kids by the way she

played with LuAnne," Carolyn said. "I think they both enjoyed it."

"When *is* Aunt Lil coming back?" the ever alert LuAnne asked plaintively.

"Well, her last letter said she was eating better and feeling much stronger," Auntie Betty answered. "We'll have to pray that they will be back soon."

The next afternoon they had a couple of "visitors" who also encouraged them to spend the rest of their money, "while you can." They told the prisoners who had not filled out all their request-for-release papers to do so at once.

"Are we going home?" Norm demanded, but they ignored the question.

"When will the Phillipses be back?" Paul asked, and again no response.

"Have you found any information about my husband?" Betty inquired. This got a rise out of them.

"I've heard the story about your husband," one replied. "We deny such a thing ever happened. We are the People's Revolutionary Government; we would never do such a thing."

"But I was there," Betty protested. "I saw him taken off into the jungle." She was dismissed with an icy stare.

As usual, they were left without receiving any definite information about anything, but they felt certain something was in the works.

A couple of days later Jay burst into the house with surprising news. "They're going to separate us!"

"Separate us? How? What do you mean?" the others demanded.

"I just heard that the Americans would be leaving soon."

"Are you sure?" Betty questioned.

"Well, as sure as we ever are about anything around here."

The matter appeared settled the next day when a guard came and ordered the Americans to present themselves at the commander's office. "Mrs. Phillips is now able to travel," the CO said. "She and her husband will be returning tomorrow. So you Americans will make preparations to leave."

Betty was thrilled to hear that Lil was better, but the thought of being separated from the others was dismaying. Especially leaving her Alliance colleagues, the Johnsons.

"Oh, Betty, how can I make it without you?" Joan wailed when she was given the news.

"I don't want to leave you either," Betty replied. "That was the first thing that crossed my mind. You'll be the only woman with all these men. You need some women with you. You're like my daughter. I really don't want to leave you."

The men took the news more pragmatically and tried to deduce what was in the making.

"They're probably going to take us north to Hanoi," Paul reasoned, "since our government would now have no official relations with Vietnam."

"And they'll take us to Saigon," Peter presumed, "since our governments already have channels open. Perhaps they'll send us right home."

"What a beautiful thought," Norm sighed.

"If that's true, and it more than likely is, how about taking some letters for our loved ones?" John asked.

"Well, sure," Norm replied seriously, "but you guys will be released soon, too, don't you think?"

"Who knows?" John shrugged.

There was a scurrying to dig out paper and pencils.

Carolyn began writing, then paused. "Norm, while you and Joan are on tour telling of all your experiences, be sure to mention those of us left behind," she teased.

Norm frowned pretentiously. "No way. If we ever get home, I'm never going to tell about any of this. I'm going to crawl into a hole and forget it ever happened."

Carolyn smiled and went on writing.

184 / Prisoners of Hope

Meanwhile Betty had been going through her suitcase. "Now, Joan, I want you to have this blouse," she declared, "and let's see what else will fit."

"Betty, I don't need a thing. Really."

"But you don't have enough clothes," Betty insisted. "I can't leave without giving you some of my things."

"But you need them yourself."

"No, no, I have plenty." And she continued going through her belongings, pulling out whatever she felt Joan might be able to use. Aware that the sharing was an expression of love, Joan accepted the offerings.

The Phillipses walked in about supper time the next day. Dick looked good, Lil vastly improved. To celebrate the reunion and also John's birthday, which would be the next day, August 15, they made doughnuts. Two apiece, the most delicious to date.

Betty could hardly sleep. She felt positive Archie awaited her. They had been issued a month's ration, so it would be a long trip. It had to be Hanoi, she anticipated. Archie would be there.

The next morning they had a tearful, emotional goodbye as the group divided. Joan didn't want to look as the other women climbed into the truck. She dreaded being left as the only woman. And she feared that the Americans might be facing a much longer captivity. After five months together, except for hospital stays, she and everyone else wished to be released as one group.

The creaky old Russian truck pulled out with the Americans at 8:15 and they reached a military barracks in Quinhon on the coast at 4:30 that afternoon. The ramshackled buildings looked desolate and abandoned, but the American POWs were too tired and dusty to be fussy. They were quickly shown to adjoining rooms, one for the men, the other for the women and LuAnne. Neither room looked inviting. Sheets of plywood, flat on the floor, were to serve as beds.

After washing up, they were presented room service. Fresh chicken, soup, vegetables, and even eggs. The polite service seemed as strange as the delicious food.

"They're really treating us like guests," Carolyn commented to the men through a hole in the wall of the small house. "Maybe we're not POWs anymore."

The men hoped she was right.

After the cold, rainy weather at Fat City, Quinhon was uncomfortably hot and confining. The prisoners were not allowed out of their rooms. They could go only to the outhouses, equipped with pails. Vietnamese women soldiers brought buckets of water for bathing and washing.

The big surprise came when they were told the truck had been sent back for the others.

"Why didn't they come with us?" Paul asked.

"Oh, you weren't supposed to be separated. There was a misinterpretation of orders," the political officer replied. "You were all supposed to come."

John sat shaking his head in puzzlement. "Who will ever believe this comedy of errors?"

They did not know what was coming off.

Their meals continued excellent. But the month's rations for traveling were taken away, along with their Vietnamese money. They were to turn in a shopping list of items they felt would be needed. They requested soap, aspirin, candles, matches, candy, and fans.

Then in an empty building across the road from their house the "interviews" began. Betty received one of the toughest grillings as she sat on the floor facing two English-speaking political officers.

They started by asking the standard questions: Name? How long in Vietnam? Your agency? Your reason for coming to Vietnam?

Of course, Betty inquired about Archie. And naturally, they denied that their soldiers of the glorious revolution had taken him. But they accepted her testimony that she had seen him abducted and went on from there.

"Why didn't you go home afterwards?" one probed.

"Why should I? That wouldn't have helped anything," she parried. "Besides, I felt needed. I had a job to do for the Lord. And I wanted to be here when Archie was released."

When the interrogation ended, it was plain they did not understand.

Each of the others had a turn. Only LuAnne escaped being questioned. She was being entertained by Lil who told her Dew Drop stories and played games with her. But after a while she got tired and began to complain of being cooped up.

The guards bent the rules and let her play on the porch. There she made friends with an older Vietnamese officer sitting in a hammock. He spoke no English and she was shy about using the smattering of Vietnamese words she had picked up in camps. But she was soon in the hammock with him, learning Communist revolutionary songs.

One afternoon when Betty was changing the bandage on Lil's painful carbuncles and Carolyn was washing clothes in a small basin, through the open window they heard a rousing quartet singing "I'm on the Battlefield for My Lord."

For an instant the three ladies froze, hardly believing what they were hearing.

"They must be picking up the Far Eastern Broadcasting Company station from Manila," Lil murmured in amazement. "Isn't it beautiful?"

A trumpet solo followed, and as they drank in the delightful sounds, scarcely breathing, they prayed silently that the *bo doi* would not move the dial.

Then as the announcer was telling about how the trumpeter had dedicated his talents to the Lord, the frequency was switched back to Radio Hanoi.

The few minutes had been like fresh air in a dungeon!

This was a day for treats. They received a package of popsicles. Tasteless, but delightfully cooling.

Then LuAnne's squeal announced the best treat of all, "Here they are!" Running to the door, they saw their friends climbing out of the truck.

Already Norm had seen the little girl. "LuAnne," he shouted in a daze, "what are you doing here?"

Norm, Joan, Peter, Ike, and Bog were never more surprised. Joan got a big hug from Betty, while Norm stared vacantly. "I can't believe this, I just can't," he kept muttering. "What are we doing here?"

"We're all going together," Paul informed them.

"Separating us was all a mistake," Dick explained. "The order was, 'Bring the Americans,' and naturally they followed orders literally, but they really wanted all of us."

"This is too much," Norm said. "You mean *we* are going to Hanoi?"

"We haven't been told, but from what we can piece together we are certain we are going north, but where else?"

The group was glad to be together but bitterly disappointed that they weren't on their way home. They spent the night there in Quinhon and left early the next morning.

Together again, the thirteen foreigners climbed into the back of the truck with several guards, their belongings, and some firewood. This truck had a tarp over the top and the prisoners were instructed not to peek out under the edges. Then the back flap was let down and they started off with a roar.

The idea of a long trip enclosed in the hot, airless truck bed was disheartening to everyone but Betty. Her heart was singing, "I'm going to Archie! I'm going to Archie!"

188 / Prisoners of Hope

"Archie"

11

"Guests" in North Vietnam

The guards disliked being inside the stuffy enclosed truck as much as the prisoners did. As soon as they were a safe distance from the Quinhon camp the *bo doi* rolled up the back tarp to let in the fresh air. Now they could breathe and see where they were going.

They were headed along the coastline up Route One, a familiar road for the veteran Alliance missionaries who once had colleagues stationed in towns along the way. Around noon they rolled into Quang Ngai where a lunch of *luong kho,* a dried protein, was distributed at a teachers' training center. Flags were flying and slogans emphasizing "independence and freedom" under Communism were displayed.

After lunch they drove on north past Hoi An and the big port of Danang where pioneer Alliance missionary R. A. Jaffray had begun evangelical work over sixty years before. Peering from the back of the truck at the Communist flags and proclamations, the missionaries' mixed emotions included the awareness that the Vietnamese believers would now have only their prayer support.

Betty had developed a boil in a most undignified place, which made the long ride in the hard metal truck bed even more painful. But she didn't mind. Each mile, she felt, was bringing her closer to Archie and the fulfillment of her thirteen-year dream of reunion.

They slept that night in a camp north of Danang. The beds were only doors laid across carpenters' "horses." But they were glad to stretch out anywhere.

The next morning they rumbled through the high "Pass of the Clouds" on the Hue highway. Here, Betty recalled, the English missionary John Haywood had been mysteriously riddled with bullets while on a trip to get supplies for leprosy patients at the hospital near Danang. He was one of eleven evangelical missionaries who had given their lives since Archie had been taken.

"And the number of Vietnamese believers who have died for Christ cannot even be counted," she informed the others.

From the pass they could see waves splashing against rocks on the sandy beach far below. It looked beautiful and deceptively peaceful.

Beyond Hue, the old imperial capital, they went into the embattled area where John and Carolyn had worked among the Bru before following a colony of tribal refugees south to Banmethuot.

Crossing the Demilitarized Zone between North and South Vietnam brought no change in scenery. Devastation was as terrible on one side as on the other. The only difference was that they saw no more open churches. On the north side Catholic and Protestant sanctuaries were boarded up, and even the Buddhist places were closed, with many in ruins.

Later in the afternoon the truck stopped. The guards got out, closed the flap, and warned them not to speak. For two hours they sat in the stifling hot "oven" until told they could get out.

Their first night in North Vietnam was spent in a house inside a military camp. Here they felt keenly the pangs of being far from home. Except Betty. She felt closer to Archie.

The next morning they had a fresh truck and driver. The ride was becoming more and more uncomfortable to Betty physically, but she was also becoming more excited. Whenever they slowed down or stopped at a town, crowds milled around them, asking questions, wanting to talk to them, but the guards strictly forbade this.

They slept that night on the floor of a prison camp and the next day boarded a "luxury" vehicle—a bus. Before leaving, dark papers were inserted over the windows to "protect" them from curious onlookers. A tarp was dropped behind the driver so no one would know the bus was carrying white-skinned foreigners. Then, incongruously, the guards permitted LuAnne to sit up front by them so she could see. Certainly her fair skin, blue eyes, and blond hair would attract anyone's attention. The Vietnamese logic was sometimes difficult to fathom.

Along the way the driver halted to let a slender, sandaled Vietnamese political officer on board. About five foot six, he was a bit taller than most Vietnamese. He wore clean gray cotton pants and a white shirt that was open at the neck. This mysterious stranger knew their names and spoke excellent English. They called him "Mr. Frankly and Sincerely" after one of his favorite phrases.

Betty could not sit straight now because of the boil. But her tippy position enabled her to see through an opening between the paper and window, and she watched the road signs with increasing interest as the bus moved along.

Betty began to notice signposts indicating "Sontay." Her throat tightened. "Sontay! Why, of course, that's where Archie is. In Sontay, the very place we were assigned so many years ago." It all seemed clear—the Lord had arranged it so that Archie had been serving in his assigned place despite war and Communism and all other impossibilities.

Her heart leaped. "Now I'm coming to him. Oh, thank You, Lord. Thank You for Your goodness and mercy and lovingkindness. Thank You for bringing me to Archie."

In midafternoon they stopped and the prisoners were escorted to the large office of the camp commander where they were told to make themselves comfortable while they were being served tea. The oriental custom made them hopeful that this would be a more pleasant stay than in previous camps.

The camp commander welcomed them. "You are here as our guests. We will do all possible to make you comfortable. However, we will need your cooperation. There are a few rules that we must inform you of.

"First, there is one American prisoner here, but you must not speak to him . . ."

Though the CO was still talking, Betty became engrossed with her thoughts. "He *is* here! I knew Archie would be here. Oh, thank You, Lord! I don't even care if I can't talk to him. Just to see him! Oh, Lord, just to see him and know he's here and he's all right.

"Oh, I wish I could have had my hair done," she thought, smoothing her long tresses that she had pulled back and tied at the neck with a strip of ribbon. "I wish I could be all fixed up and wearing a pretty new dress. But he doesn't care. I know he loves me no matter how I look.

"But then he's gotten older, too. I'll bet he's really bald by now. But that's not important. I wonder how long it will be before we can talk with each other. Be alone. Until we can hold each other."

The CO was droning on about camp regulations, but Betty couldn't collect her thoughts enough to listen. Her one concern was to see the "American prisoner."

Though impatient, she did try to be realistic. "Who else could he be? The military prisoners were discharged in 1972. The American forces left then, so he couldn't be a soldier captured since. And all us foreigners who were captured during the final offensive were brought together some time ago. No, he would have to be a long-time prisoner. Besides, the Lord had a purpose in allowing me to be captured. What else could it be, but to reunite me with Archie?"

After about a half hour the meeting was dismissed and the prisoners escorted to their quarters. Some of the prison guards had to smile at the unmilitary bearing of the bedraggled crew of foreigners. They straggled in, gawking at their new surroundings, looking more like a group of dirty tourists than prisoners of war.

From the main office they walked toward a long cement building. "This first room is for the single men," they were told, "the next three are for the couples. Mrs. Mitchell, your room is over this way."

"Oh, but I want to stay with the others," she protested.

And just then, across the way standing next to the building where her room was to be, she caught sight of the American prisoner. The tall, dark, clean-cut looking young man was watching them with open curiosity.

"It isn't Archie! Archie's not here." Betty couldn't accept it. "He has to be here. '*One* American prisoner.'" The reminder came unbidden. In her confusion she realized that she was being led away from the other prisoners.

"But I don't want to be by myself," she complained. "I want to stay with the others." Her objections were in vain. She was deposited in a small room with one tiny window and narrow, short cot.

"Are they punishing me for peeking out the bus window?" she fretted. "Is this to be solitary confinement? Won't I be with my friends? Archie isn't here, and now I don't have my friends either! Lord, I can't take this."

She collapsed by the tiny undersized cot, sobbing. All the pain and hurt and disappointments of the past years flooded over her and she cried out, "Lord, help me."

But one dismaying thought kept reverberating in her brain: "Archie isn't here. Archie isn't here." She tried to regain control of her emotions, but doubts flooded her mind. "If Archie isn't here, then where is he? Maybe he is dead after all. Perhaps all my years of waiting have been in vain. Lord Jesus," she called out in anguish, "why? Why did You allow me to get my hopes up? Why did You allow me to be captured? Why isn't he here?"

The thoughts continued to assail her as she knelt alone in her solitary room until, much later, a knock came at the door. "You may go to the kitchen and bring food back to your room." She followed as if in a trance.

In the kitchen she learned a suspicious fact about the sleeping arrangements. There was a vacant room next to the Johnsons. Why wasn't she put there, unless there was a specific reason for keeping her separate from the others?

She returned to her lonely room too disappointed to try the food. It grew dark outside and she tried to sleep. She tossed and turned, but the boil made it impossible for her to be comforable on the short, lumpy bed.

Even more tormenting was the spiritual battle that raged within. She was ashamed that she had murmured and complained about the room assigned to her.

Finally, in deep contrition she was able to pray, "Father, forgive me for breaking my vow not to complain. Help me to trust You, to serve You."

Suddenly the tiny prison was transformed by the presence of

the Comforter from a terrible, confining dungeon to a glorious abode. "It's all right, Betty," the still, small Voice assured her. "I forgive you. I love you. I am with you and will never leave you alone."

A deep peace flooded her soul and she was able to sleep.

The next morning she felt physically ill. But Lil came, and then Joan, to help her. They got some oral penicillin to help heal the boil. Knowing that her friends had access to her room and that she was free to visit theirs reassured her that she had not been separated from the others as a punishment. They had assigned her a smaller room merely because she was alone.

At the first opportunity Betty went to apologize to Mr. Khoi, the officer to whom she had complained. "I am sorry for the way I acted when I was put in a building separate from the others," she told the bland-faced Vietnamese.

"That's all right," he said, shrugging his shoulders. "It doesn't make any difference."

"Oh, yes, it does," she insisted, "because I am God's child and He showed me that I was wrong to complain. That's why I want you to know I am sorry."

The dumbfounded Communist could think of no reply to that startling statement, but Betty, because she had been obedient to God, felt confident that it would one day open the way for her to witness to this man.

As another token of God's loving care her longing for fruit was satisfied abundantly. In her diary she called August 24 a "six-banana day." The day was further special because it was Becki's twenty-seventh birthday. To be back in North Vietnam where Becki had spent most of her first two years made Betty remember what a sweet, happy child her firstborn had been.

It was soon evident that some official decision had been made about them, although, of course, they were never informed what this was. Their every need was now being duly considered and, if possible, fulfilled. The food was greatly improved. They even had bread for the first time, along with citrus fruits for Vitamin C. They got hats and additional clothing—each of the women received two pairs of dark blue pants and flowered material for blouses—and medical treatment and medicines as needed. Betty's request for a longer bed was granted to her great relief and comfort.

Betty used some of her blouse material to make a curtain for her tiny window. She hung it and stepped back to admire the transformation created in her cell-like room. It did make the room a little homey.

And Carolyn used some of her cloth to make matching mu-mu sleepwear for herself and LuAnne. The privacy to change into comfortable sleeping clothes was a welcome luxury.

Both men and women had bath houses and could take as many baths a day as they wished. What a treat to be able to keep cool and clean during the torrid weather. The oriental-style ablutions called for lathering all over with soap, then rinsing off with water from a bucket. Not quite up to Western standards, but it beat dunking in a river.

Another source of pleasure was a small circulating library of books. They got Taylor Caldwell's fictionalized biography of Luke, several Russian novels, and *Today's English Version* of the New Testament.

"Frankly and sincerely," their escort said, "we have tried to find books acceptable to you." He seemed to recognize that the interests of the missionaries might be different from those of some of the other prisoners.

But the most delightful addition to their confinement was a brownish-black, short-haired puppy with spots of white. The little short-eared canine won their hearts immediately. Though he belonged to one of the guards, he soon learned that he got a lot more attention from the prisoners and began spending all his time entertaining them.

Norm started calling him "Budo" in memory of the dog he and Joan had had to abandon in Banmethuot. The name caught on, and soon even the guards called him Budo. The mysterious American they had nicknamed "Slim" had been teaching the pup some tricks and the newcomers joined in.

Norm threw a stick, and Budo caught on to retrieving immediately. Soon he was catching it on the fly and racing back. Never having seen a dog do that trick before, the guards were suitably impressed. But they were not the least impressed when the puppy began hunching his back and growling every time one of the Vietnamese came near the prisoners' quarters. He was supposed to help guard the prisoners, not protect them!

Their spirits were rising again. All the good treatment and the friendliness of Mr. Frankly and Sincerely had to mean something. After he took the unprecedented step of identifying himself as "Mr. Van," Norm ventured to ask when they would be going home.

"Just try to be patient," he replied. "Maybe six months—that's not long."

"A year is a long time to be separated from our children," Lil moaned. "Can't you give us a date?"

"No, I can't do that. Just trust me. I tell you frankly and sincerely, you will be going soon."

Norm's face reddened under his dark beard. "We've been told that all along. Why should we believe you now?"

Mr. Van's face clouded. "Ah, you make me sad when you don't believe me. I tell the truth. I never lie."

On Labor Day the POWs had another surprise. Speakers were installed in each room so they could hear music and English programs. That evening at nine o'clock the missionaries caught the familiar strains of "I Love to Tell the Story," introducing the Back to the Bible broadcast over FEBC. They paid rapt attention to the program that included a message about why missionaries went abroad.

When the program ended they hoped to hear a news broadcast, but the set was turned off. "You wouldn't want to hear that," Mr. Van said patronizingly. "You know, I listen to this station frequently," he added. "It has helped me learn many English idioms and has also improved my pronunciation because they speak very clearly."

The next day was an important date for the North Vietnamese. It commemorated the time in 1945 when Ho Chi Minh had vowed in Hanoi to unify all Vietnam, declaring, "There is nothing more precious than freedom and independence."

"Now we are victorious at last!" Mr. Van bragged. "The Americans had everything and we had nothing, but we won. Yes, we won. Now the Americans must listen to us. They must recognize us, for we have defeated them."

The crowing was hard to take, but they felt silence would be the better part of valor at this point. They worked off some of their pent-up emotions playing catch with one of the Millers' tennis balls for an hour or so.

Later, an area of the courtyard between the buildings was marked off for a volleyball court. Betty's court powers surprised those who hadn't known her well. Though the oldest of the group, she had excellent coordination and still excelled as an athlete. And she played hard because she liked to win.

Slim was allowed to play as long as he didn't speak. They became more and more curious and often speculated about who their fellow captive might be. But they didn't dare talk while the omnipresent *bo doi* hovered around to enforce the communication ban.

The improved treatment included medical exams at a nearby

hospital. Joan had been suffering severe headaches and Lil's leg was badly swollen. Bog had a tooth pulled. Trips to the hospital were made in an uncovered jeep. Just to see people going about their daily tasks gave them a lift. Everyone seemed busy; all the streets and roads were immaculate.

Offsetting the improved treatment were the intense interrogation sessions. They soon had names for the different inquisitors and learned which ones would give them a hard time. The sessions followed a pattern. First one of them, or sometimes a couple, would be called in, without advance warning. They would sit across a table from the interrogator, with an interpreter at the side. Then they would be served strong tea from a little teapot.

The interrogator would pour a little, maybe a half cup, and ask, "Who are you? Why did you come to Vietnam?"

Perhaps the most astute questioner was "Baldy." When questioning couples he would ask one a question, then watch the other's reaction to the answer. Often he would quickly scribble something down on paper, as if he had caught them in some contradiction.

He would zero in on political issues, such as the Pentagon Papers, which he had read, but none of the Americans had. He knew much more about the American political scene than the missionaries who lived a half world away from their homeland. But he never seemed to believe they were not withholding information.

"We're just not politically motivated," Carolyn kept telling him.

"I'm sure. And the CIA never visited you?"

"Well, they would come by, of course. We were the only Americans around, and they would just come to visit."

"What would you talk about?"

"Oh, our families, where we lived back home, how long

since we had been to the States, and recent news we had. That sort of thing."

"Certainly," he laughed. "And you never gave information about troop movements?"

"Troop movements? We didn't know anything about troop movements. They would have known more about that than we did. We'd tell them about the Bru, their culture and customs, language. But we'd talk to anybody about that," John protested.

"That's all we could tell them," Carolyn agreed. "We could never make political statements because we are nonpolitical. We didn't come to Vietnam for political reasons, we came to share the Word of God with the Bru people. And that's all we did do."

But Baldy was never satisfied.

"Why did you Americans rush to Mr. Struharick's home and the Canadians didn't?" he asked during different interrogations.

"We would have gone if we could," the Johnsons tried to convince him. "The troops invaded the Raday village before we could get out. All of us had planned to meet at Paul's, and we would have if it had been possible."

Baldy's sneer made them feel like liars even though they were telling the truth.

"Tell me, Mr. Struharick," he asked Paul one day, "you know your way around in the jungle; why didn't you try to escape from Banmethuot or from one of the camps?"

"With that bunch?" Paul exploded. "You think I was going to try to lead those greenhorns through the jungle?"

Even Baldy had to laugh at that. The unmilitary conduct of the foreigners was a source of amusement to all the Communist officers.

Paul wasn't amused, however, at the continual badgering about his "American wife."

"I have only one wife," he declared. "Her name is H'Lum. She is a Raday tribeswoman, but she is my wife, and I love her. She is also the mother of my only son, who will soon have his first birthday, and I want to see him."

"It is not unusual for white men to take tribeswomen as wives while in Vietnam, but they always return to white wives."

"H'Lum is my one and only wife. When I return to the States she will go with me."

"Where is she now?"

"I wish I knew. She was in Bangkok when I was captured. And I assure you when I'm released I'll find her."

The interpreters were sometimes thrown by Peter's vocabulary and manner of speech. One day Mr. Khoi asked why he, as an Australian, was at the USAID house. "Well, I had come to Banmethuot to visit the radio station, but for courtesy's sake I stopped to see Mr. Struharick."

"Courtesy's sake. Who is Mr. Courtesy? I have heard nothing of him. Why hasn't anyone mentioned him before?" he demanded.

Then Peter had to explain and explain that there was no "Mr. Courtesy."

But the worst interrogations were about the children, especially for the mothers who found it difficult to hold down their feelings. When Lil's replies didn't please Baldy one day he snarled, "You just don't want to see your children again!"

"Oh, but I do!" she cried. "I want to see my children. I do want to see my children!" She broke down and sobbed uncontrollably, leaving the embarrassed inquisitor not knowing what to do with the weeping woman.

After a long silence he finally said, "Well, you mothers will be reunited with your children, won't you?"

"But when?" she asked. "How much longer must we wait?" But, of course, she was given no information.

Everyone dreaded being questioned by "The Axe," one of the toughest interrogators. When Betty staggered out of the interrogation room one day after he was through with her, Lil noticed her wiping away tears and trying to collect her shattered composure. She whispered to Joan, "That breaks my heart. You know how much control Betty has. To make her cry, he must have really been mean."

"I'll say," Joan agreed. "If they can break her, they can break anyone."

"He'd ask me things I couldn't remember," Betty explained. "Like who was the leader of the Alliance missionaries when we came to the field twenty-seven years ago. Then when I'd try to think back, he'd shout, 'Why are you hesitating? If you tell the truth, you do not need to hesitate! Don't take time to think up lies, just tell the truth.'

"I tried to convince him that I always tell the truth, that I never lie, but of course he didn't believe me."

"He's a tough one all right," Norm agreed, trying to console Betty. "We'll have to pray that he gets moved out of here."

"Let's add 'Blue Shirt' to the list of undesirables," John suggested. They were relieved when those two were removed from the camp.

Dick came back one day and said he'd been told what his crime was. The others gathered around to hear. None of them had ever managed to get such information.

"I'm too good," Dick smiled. "I was told, 'Mr. Phillips, you are just too good. You will make people think all Americans are good.' So that's my sin."

In trying to learn what her crime was, Betty told one interrogator, "All I can think of is that my crime is being an American. You always talk about hating Americans, but I can't help being an American. And if that is my sin, you will just have to hate me."

"Oh, no. We don't hate all Americans."

"Well, then, my sin must be being a Christian, because all I ever did in Vietnam was to try to love and teach the gospel of Jesus Christ. But I can't understand that because you say you have religious freedom."

"Oh, we have religious freedom," he insisted. "You just don't understand what religious freedom means." But he didn't bother to present the Communist viewpoint on that matter.

As the questionings increased in number and intensity the missionaries prayed all the more earnestly for those closeted in the interrogation room. One answer to this prayer came in an unexpected form. About a month after their arrival a truck drove into camp with a cow in it. Their first thought was, "We're going home and the cow is for a goodbye feast."

It turned out this was a bit overoptimistic, but "Bossy" did prove to be a blessing. Allowed the run of the camp, she would often wander into the interrogation room and "do her duty." The following morning the interrogators found the stench too much for them and so the grillings had to be delayed while guards cleaned up the mess and aired out the room. This happened so often that Norm dubbed the animal "The Holy Cow," for she was a means of answering their prayers. As far as the foreigners were concerned anything that meant less time for interrogations was a blessing.

During this era of "The Holy Cow" Betty woke one night with a hard chill that hung on for an hour. The day before she had felt great and had played two strenuous games of volleyball, but by morning she was running a fever and felt tired out—a recurrence of malaria. The medic started her on a regimen of medicine at once, but that made her vomit so the next day he gave her shots instead.

One day while Betty suffered from malaria, God spoke to her heart concerning Archie: "You must not worry about him. You know he would never deny Me; he is in My will. It isn't really important where he is physically, as long as he is in My will."

Once more the Everlasting Arms enfolded her and gave her peace. A peace that in her circumstances could only be miraculous. "Remember," the Voice told her, "he would never deny Me. And that's more important than knowing exactly where he is at any moment."

The chills and fever persisted on and off. She had an excruciating headache and no desire for food, and she could not keep liquids down. Continual wretching made her stomach extremely sore. The medic, Joan, and Lil did all they could for her and still she was no better. Betty asked the Christians to pray for her healing and anoint her according to Scripture, as they had done on numerous other occasions during the captivity.

Mr. Van noticed the gathering in Betty's small room and came to investigate.

"What's going on?" he asked Peter, who was standing outside. "Is something wrong?"

"Oh, no. They do this every once in a while when someone is sick. They all put their hands on the patient and anoint them with some oily salve and they pray. I don't quite understand it all, but you know, it really seems to make a difference."

The political officer looked puzzled, but didn't interfere. Since he was responsible for the group, he felt it his duty to know what went on, but he also tried to be friendly toward the prisoners. Of all the officers, he was the "nice guy." The captives kidded with him, but never completely forgot that he was playing the part he had been assigned.

He kept commenting on how much time the missionaries spent reading their Bibles and one day asked to borrow one. From statements he made after returning the Bible, they could tell he had read some, but he never showed interest in a personal relationship with God.

Mr. Van planned a birthday party for LuAnne on September

"Guests" in North Vietnam / 205

16, the day after Betty's anointing. He brought gifts—a little watering can and play scales. Carolyn made some doll clothes. "Uncle" Peter carved a fish to wear on a chain. "Uncle" Ike fashioned a pendant. "Auntie" Lil drew a picture. The Johnsons gave a bottle containing a few drops of precious perfume.

The camp commander had brought out a birthday cake from Hanoi, carefully packed in a tin. He said that in all North Vietnam only one hotel made such cakes. To add to the importance of LuAnne's big day, an entourage of high officials was on hand from Hanoi to make pictures. The prisoners did not quite know what to make of all the special treatment, but the happy LuAnne was oblivious to any ulterior motives.

After the party she ran to show "Auntie" Betty her presents. Betty was still weak, but had not lost her food one time since they had prayed for her the night before. She even managed to successfully down a cup of coffee. In the next days of improvement she was given lots of fruit and the medic surprised her with a big custard apple. Her fever went steadily down as the week progressed.

It took another week to get back her strength. She was sitting outside the Johnsons' room sunning herself one day when one of the minor political officers came up and started talking to her. Soon Betty was sharing how Christ had changed her life, and he was telling of the transformation that came through the revolution. He maintained that Communists did not need God.

"Well, I want to tell you about Him anyway," Betty persisted. "Because one day you will have to stand before Him in judgment, and I want you to remember that you had this opportunity to hear about Him."

The other prisoners were milling about, listening to the conversation. Peter laughed, "Listen to that. One fanatic to another!"

But the missionaries didn't care if they were considered fanatics. They didn't know if they would ever be permitted to return home or to another field of service, so they took every opportunity to witness. During interrogations the inevitable question, Why did you come to Vietnam? provided opportunity to tell what Christ had done in their lives and why they had come to share this good news with others.

Norm saw this as not only a chance to share the gospel, but a way of using up the time of an interrogator. He would give directions for studying the Bible, exegete whole passages, rattle off sermon outlines, teach lessons he had taught at the Raday Bible school. In explaining God's leadership one day to Baldy, he said, "I know this is hard for you to understand, but—"

"Oh, but I do understand," Baldy insisted. Norm didn't argue, but found it rather strange that the Communists never would admit they didn't understand something.

Mr. Van gave them one exception to this when he came by to borrow the Millers' "screwturner."

"One thing I do not comprehend about Americans," he admitted, "you have such a fixation about bodies. We get much pressure about your MIAs. My own brother went South for a big battle four years ago and never came back. So we know he must be dead, but we are not concerned about where his body is. Why is this so important to Americans?"

"It's the uncertainty," Betty explained. "As long as we don't know for certain a person is dead, then hope lingers on that the loved one might be alive somewhere in a prison camp. I'm sure our families feel that way about us now, and I certainly feel that way about my husband. I would like so very much to know exactly what has happened to him."

"I tell you frankly and sincerely, Mrs. Mitchell, your husband is dead. If he were alive, I would know about it. It would be my responsibility to know."

"Then can't you get me some facts and dates?" she begged.

"I know you Vietnamese keep excellent records about everything. Surely if he died in a prison camp somewhere, there is a record of that fact."

"I will try to find out for you," he promised.

Betty was encouraged. If she could not be reunited with Archie, perhaps she could at least get some definite word about him.

The prisoners continued to have their hopes built up and then torn down. When Bossy came they thought surely that meant they would be released soon, but after two weeks nothing had happened. When their U.S. currency was returned to them near the end of September they took this as good news, but days went by and still no word.

Betty was sitting in her room writing in her diary one day when Budo came and licked her foot. The friendly little pup made her smile. He was a gift of enjoyment to all the prisoners.

Then she wrote: *Last day of September. This month has gone quickly. Only wonder when the release date.*

12

Answered Prayers

"How would you enjoy a sight-seeing tour of Hanoi?" Mr. Van asked.

"Yeah, sure, Mr. Van. You and I can go live it up awhile," Norm shot back.

"No, this time I am not teasing. A bus is coming this afternoon. We can leave early in the morning and spend the whole day visiting museums and other places of interest."

The prisoners could hardly believe it.

A bus did arrive later that day, and on Friday morning at 6:30 they took off. There were no covers on the windows, and they traveled along in a real holiday atmosphere.

Coming into the area of Hanoi, Betty was surprised to see little improvement in the twenty-five years since her last visit. In 1949 and '50 the city had been recovering from World War II, but there were far more shops than they saw now. As they drove along broad tree-lined boulevards she noted that French provincial architecture still predominated.

Sidewalks and streets were crowded with people walking or riding bicycles. Yet the scene was enveloped in a strange, subdued silence. The few motorized vehicles were either military or official.

They saw no visible war damage, no destruction at all. The people looked poor, but industrious. Every piece of available ground had something growing on it. Rice or vegetables, and occasionally flowers.

They noticed no large markets, such as Betty remembered, and only a few shops for bread or meat. Many shoppers clustered around these, trying to purchase supplies. There were no dogs on the streets. Mr. Van explained that they were outlawed as unsanitary.

When the bus stopped and they trooped out, the people were curious and very friendly. The foreigners were puzzled by this in view of the war, until they realized the Vietnamese thought they were Russian tourists.

Mr. Van led them into the imposing Museum of the Revolution where they listened to lectures on the exhibits. As they strolled along a corridor, Officer Khoi shadowed Slim to make sure he didn't talk to the other prisoners. Slim paid little attention to his bodyguard and occasionally wandered away from him.

When Mr. Khoi, not the brightest of the Communist officers, realized his charge had slipped away, he would dash over and stand beside him.

"Mr. Khoi, this is where I was taken," Slim said loudly as he pointed to a large photograph of Phan Rang.

The others were all ears. "Where? Where was that?"

"Oh, he was captured in Phan Rang," someone replied.

"Come on," Mr. Khoi muttered disgustedly, pulling Slim toward the next exhibit.

Most impressive was a dramatic reenactment of the capture of Saigon, complete with sounds of battle and smoke that drifted away as a tiny helicopter lifted off from a paper-mache American Embassy. A voice through a loudspeaker proudly announced: "Vietnam is now totally liberated and free of foreign forces." A parade of miniature tanks bearing the flags of the National Liberation Front and the North Vietnamese drove through the center of Saigon, accompanied by the strains of a military march.

Next the prisoners were taken to an art museum that featured not only atheistic masterpieces, but also diagrams of ancient wars and dramatic scenes in which Vietnamese were shown fighting off foreign invaders. The guide's voice swelled as he told them proudly, "Every time we won the war we sent the aggressors home, for we want no foreigners here."

The prisoners broke into cheers and clapping. "Hurrah, they send all foreigners home!" The shout echoed through the marble halls as one by one the group latched onto the phrase. Mr. Van shook his head, embarrassed at the demeanor of his charges, but he couldn't keep from laughing.

After the tour they were served a delicious meal in a private house. For dessert, Mr. Khoi treated them with popsicles.

Norm yelled out, "Khoi for President!" Khoi hung his head in embarrassment and the rest cheered. Being treated like guests was so exhilarating to the prisoners after months of POW humiliation that they laughed and joked hilariously.

The rest of the day's tour was one continuous lark.

As they were walking along a busy street Mr. Van noticed that Joan held her Raday shoulder bag closed with her hand.

"Jo-an," he called with his usual mispronunciation, "why do you hold your purse so close? No one will steal anything from you."

"But, Mr. Van," Norm responded in mock seriousness,

"she has to be very careful, for all our escape plans are in that bag. We can't lose that!"

"Oh, Norman," Mr. Van laughed, "you are always kidding."

Riding back to Sontay, the group sang and joked contentedly. They felt positive they would be released. The only possible motive for the delightful outing was to give them a happy experience to tell about when they got home.

But as soon as they returned to their rooms they realized their own naivete. Their quarters had been ransacked. Every possession, every book, every piece of paper—absolutely all their belongings—had been thoroughly inspected. Their beds had been taken apart, literally, and moved from off the "horses."

Norm was indignant. He called Mr. Van, "Here you take us out and give us a wonderful time to create good feelings, then your comrades go behind our backs and tear through our stuff. Why didn't you simply say, 'We are going to search your rooms'? We wouldn't have minded that. We have nothing to hide."

"Why, Norman, we would never search your rooms," Mr. Van tried to calm him. "One of the soldiers must have been curious and came in to look."

"Oh, yeah," Norm retorted, "and dumped stuff out of sugar bags and tore the beds apart. We aren't stupid enough to swallow that."

"Norm, you had better shut up," Joan cautioned softly as she placed a restraining hand on his arm.

For once Norm took his wife's advice. Mr. Van walked off.

"I really think they are playing on our emotions on purpose," the dispirited Norm confided to his wife. "First they build up our hopes and then they lower the boom on us. They're just trying to break us, but it won't work because we have nothing to hide. We have cooperated with them and told the truth about everything. I don't know any more we could do."

The next day, though designated a day of rest, the atmosphere was tense. The happy emotions of yesterday were replaced by gloom. Everyone was wearing such a long face that Betty decided to use Isaiah 12 in the Sunday worship service.

"We have plenty for which to praise the Lord. Even if we don't feel like it now, we will later," she said before reading from the Bible: *"And in that day thou shalt say, O Lord, I will praise thee: though thou wast angry with me, thine anger is turned away, and thou comfortedst me. Behold, God is my salvation; I will trust, and not be afraid: for the Lord Jehovah is my strength and my song; he also is become my salvation. Therefore with joy shall ye draw water out of the wells of salvation. And in that day shall ye say, Praise the Lord, call upon his name, declare his doings among the people, make mention that his name is exalted. Sing unto the Lord; for he hath done excellent things; this is known in all the earth. Cry out and shout, thou inhabitant of Zion: for great is the Holy One of Israel in the midst of thee."*

The six verses boosted their spirits. As they prayed, comfort and peace flooded their hearts. "When we get down again," Betty suggested, "let's just stop and ask ourselves, 'Who is really in control here anyway?' Then let's just praise the Lord."

That evening they were subjected to a long redundant lecture on the history of Vietnam, culminating with the "liberation" of Saigon. This was topped off by some breathtakingly beautiful pictures of the country. The photography was as impressive as the scenery. Mr. Van was all smiles.

They debated the meaning of the sales pitch. Did this spell the start of a subtle campaign to convert them to Communism?

Perhaps. Did their captors have their best interests at heart? Hardly.

"Remember we are in enemy hands and everything they do serves their own ends," Carolyn stressed.

"Yeah, Mr. Van is a nice guy because he's been assigned to play that part," Norm agreed. "If he were ordered to take us out and shoot us, he would. He wouldn't like it, but he'd do it."

"Any of them would," Betty spoke up, "because they're so disciplined and dedicated to their cause."

On Monday morning a car pulled up and with no warning Paul was taken out. Enroute to the vehicle he passed the Johnsons' open door. "See ya," he called hopefully.

"Where are you going?" Norm asked. "Hey, everybody, they're taking Paul away!"

Hurrying from their rooms, the foreigners asked what was happening. "Oh, he's just going for some questioning," Mr. Van assured them. "He'll be back soon."

"What do you call soon?" Peter asked, greatly upset that his friend was being taken.

"Just a couple of days," Mr. Van replied.

Paul and Mr. Khoi got into the waiting vehicle and they pulled out amid calls of goodbye. The others milled around, discussing this latest development.

"Do you think we'll ever see him again?" John asked.

"Not if we're released," Dick prophesied.

When the jeep returned shortly Jay commented, "Well, at least we know he's nearby. That was a quick trip."

"We don't know anything," Peter countered. "He might've been transferred to another vehicle just to confuse us. For that matter, he could be dead by now. We don't really know anything." The dark-haired Australian shuffled back to his room and flopped on his bunk. He and the USAID man had developed a deep friendship. He would miss him.

The interrogations were stepped up, three and four being

conducted at the same time. The interrogators leaned hard on the prisoners. "Why does your organization have two names?" the Millers were asked. "Sometimes you call yourselves Wycliffe Bible Translators and other times you are the Summer Institute of Linguistics. What motive could you have for this?"

"Because we are both," John tried to explain to the belligerent questioner. "Before you can translate the Bible into an unwritten language you must become a linguist. You have to learn the language and learn it well before you even begin to translate."

"How does your work differ from Dr. Phillips' work?"

"It doesn't. He is a translator also, and he even studied in our courses and taught one year. We do exactly the same work."

"Then why are you members of different organizations?"

"Well, we work together because we have common goals. The Alliance was in Vietnam long before Wycliffe. They invited us to come and help them. There is no competition between us."

"And just who funds all these activities?"

"Christians in the United States give support money."

"You mean they are taxed to support you?"

"Oh, no, they give voluntarily. This is besides the money they pay in taxes."

"And then, of course, you have your income from helping the CIA."

"We have never helped the CIA. We have never received money from them."

"And they just came to visit you to talk about old times," the interrogator sneered.

Meanwhile in another room Betty was being given a hard time. "Mrs. Mitchell, why didn't you go home after your husband was taken from you?"

"What good would that have done? I had a job to do in Vietnam. I felt the Lord had called me there to do it and that I should continue even if Archie was gone. Besides, I wanted to be in Banmethuot when he was returned. I expected him to come right back, just as the Viet Cong told me."

"Mrs. Mitchell, I can't understand you. You talk about God as if He is real."

"He is real! And someday you will have to stand before Him in judgment. Don't you ever think about what will happen to you when you die?"

"When I die my people will buy me a coffin, and maybe they will cry some. Then they will bury me, and that's all."

"But the Bible says that everyone, even Ho Chi Minh, will have to stand before God someday. And I know He is real and His Word is real because He changed my life, and He can change yours, too."

"You missionaries like to change people's lives, don't you? Well, now that our glorious revolution has been victorious we have no need of your religion."

The questions went on and on. Repeating the same inquiries that had been made almost since the time they had been taken.

Tension among the foreigners increased as they wondered what was going to happen next. The interrogators had tried to get Dick to sign an anti-American statement and he refused. Afterward, while Dick was still out of the room, the others speculated on why they picked on him.

"I think because he is quiet they thought he'd break," Norm supposed. "They underestimate Dick. He's steel. He'll never sign a lie."

The next morning the prisoners were called in. "All money and valuables will be confiscated for safekeeping," they were informed. "We don't want anyone going in your rooms and stealing your things."

On the way back to their rooms they grumbled among themselves that this was just an excuse for taking their valuables.

At each door guards awaited them. "We have to check all written materials," they were told. And the guards took everything with writing on it. Bibles. Books. Even a couple of pencil drawings Lil had made to give to Dick for their anniversary the next day. And the pricless Bru and Mnong Scripture manuscripts and Dick's doctoral thesis.

"Will we get them back?" Carolyn pleaded. "We've devoted fifteen years of our lives to producing those translations."

"A ninety-five percent chance you will get them back," they were told. "Now you will all begin writing your biographies. Omit nothing. We want all the details of your lives."

The whole atmosphere and the way in which orders were given seemed to have changed. They could only guess what this meant. Also, Budo had disappeared. Norm asked the guard who owned the prized pet.

"Oh, he's dead already," came the reply. "In Vietnam we have only smart dogs and meat dogs. Budo was a meat dog."

"But he was smart!" Joan wailed.

"Poor Budo," Betty lamented. "We'll miss him."

October 8, the Phillipses' anniversary, was a hard day. Grieving over their manuscripts, they were taken separately that day for interrogations. It was the hardest Lil had experienced. The Vietnamese began asking the same old questions: "What is your name? Why did you come to Vietnam?"

"Oh, what's the use in telling you?" Lil finally rebelled. "I've told you over and over and over again and you never believed me those times, and you won't believe me if I tell you again." And she broke down and cried.

Despite the tears the man insisted they continue. "You must endure one more time, Mrs. Phillips." And then he began asking her questions about Christians she knew in different villages. She didn't want to lie, but it hurt her deeply to have to incriminate the very people she had come to serve.

When she finally was allowed to leave the interrogation room her eyes were swollen and her nose red. She just couldn't seem to bring her emotions under control.

Noticing her sad state, Carolyn sought to comfort her, "Could I share something with you?" Lil nodded. "The Lord gave me a verse after a hard interview. It means a lot to me and perhaps will help you, too." She quoted softly First Peter 3:15: "Quietly trust yourself to Christ your Lord, and if anybody asks why you believe as you do, be ready to tell him, and *do it in a gentle and respectful way.*"

"That's tremendous," Lil responded. "I'm going to write it down and memorize it. Perhaps I'll even take it in with me the next time I'm called; maybe that will help."

The ever present Mr. Van had noticed the women talking and came over to see what was disturbing Lil.

"Yesterday they took our manuscripts," Lil explained. "Today is our wedding anniversary, and I had drawn two pictures to give to Dick as a present and they took those, too. You remember, you were watching me draw them the other day."

"Oh, yes. The picture of the open rose and one with writing on it and a picture of the little oil lamps we gave you. I think we could return those. Just wait, and I'll see what I can do."

On the way to see about the all-important drawings Mr. Van stuck his head in the Johnsons' doorway. "Jo-an," he asked, "what do Americans do to celebrate wedding anniversaries?"

"Oh, the husband takes the wife out for dinner," Joan shot back.

"Well, we couldn't allow that now, could we?" he smiled. "But perhaps we could arrange something."

The "something" turned out to be a surprise party in the main office. The only problem was, no one felt like having a party, least of all Dick and Lil. But they had no choice; they would have to go.

They were served bananas, candy, coffee, and tea. LuAnne had made a card, using her colored pens. It had a big blue, daisy-looking flower on the front and said HAPPY ANNIVERSARY in big block letters. On the inside she had drawn a big sun with a man and woman (stick figures) smiling broadly and had laboriously printed HAPPY ANNIVERSARY TO UNCLE DICK AND AUNT LIL. It was signed, LUANNE, OCT. 8, 1975.

"It's beautiful, LuAnne," Lil told her sincerely. "I'll keep it always."

"How long have you been married?" Mr. Van asked politely.

"Fifteen years," Dick responded.

"We were married in the little chapel at the Dalat School," Lil reminisced. "Grady Mangham, our field director, performed the ceremony. And Uncle Herbert Jackson, one of the pioneer Alliance missionaries in Vietnam, gave me away."

They talked for a while about Vietnam back in 1960 and how different things were then.

"Why don't we sing something?" Peter suggested. No one seemed very enthusiastic about singing that night, but then he added, "You know, this might be our last time together. We might all be separated."

"Yes," Betty agreed, thinking of Paul, "we might all be separated."

The singing helped to heal their battered spirits. They sang love songs, rounds, even some patriotic American songs. When they sang, "Love's Old Sweet Song" Peter was overcome with emotion, but he was too choked to explain the significance of the song to him. They were lighthearted as they went to their rooms. The expressed love and care had turned a very dark day into a lovely evening for Dick and Lil.

The next day, while they were working on their biographies,

Betty began writing about her conversion. Putting the words on paper, she relived again that time when her married sister Allie came to visit her and said she had become a Christian. "And you're going to be saved, too, Betty. I just know it. Even if you don't understand it all now."

"I really didn't understand it," Betty wrote, "and my sister had to leave before she could explain it all to me. I decided to go to church so that I might hear how to find the new life in Christ that she told me about. I visited a number of different churches, but none of the ministers told me what I wanted to hear.

"Because of the longing that was in my heart I bought a Bible and began to read, but I didn't know how to find the answers I was seeking. I just began at the beginning with the book of Genesis and that just told me about the creation of man. I even went to a Bible study, but the people there saw me walk in with my Bible and presumed I was a Christian. But I knew I wasn't.

"Then I went home one weekend to Bly, Oregon, to visit my family, and I discovered that Mr. Pollock, whom we had known in Minnesota, had begun a church in his home. In the services that Sunday he told how Christ had died for sinners. How He had paid our sin-debt so we might be forgiven if we turned to Him in faith. I trusted Him that day. He forgave my sins and gave me the new life I had longed for.

"From that time on, I have tried to serve Him and tell others about His love. And He has been with me all the way. He's never left me or forsaken me."

When Betty was eating lunch with the Johnsons she confided, "You know, I first dreaded writing my biography, but it turned out to be a great blessing. Made me thank the Lord all over for loving me enough to die for me. For saving me and giving me real purpose in life."

Betty turned in her story only to be given another assignment: write the history of The Christian and Missionary Alliance in Vietnam and name all the officers of the mission during the twenty-seven years she had served there. Dick was to write the history and organization of the Alliance worldwide, as well as in Vietnam. Norm was to tell about the Raday Bible School at Banmethuot, and John to relate the work of Wycliffe in Vietnam. None had the information needed to adequately cover the broad subjects.

The writing and the stepped-up interrogations continued through the next week. The pressure of persistent questioning and the plague of various physical problems lowered their spirits again.

Then on October 15 a bus rolled up in the afternoon. "You will enjoy another tour of Hanoi in the morning," Mr. Van informed them.

Should they be glad or sad? The varying reactions of their captors had them so confused that they really didn't know what to expect anymore.

They had an interesting day in Hanoi. They saw the oldest university, drove by the flat-roofed mausoleum containing the body of Ho Chi Minh, and visited a three-floored art museum. After lunch, served in the same house as before, they were taken to another museum where they were shown a movie on the life of Ho Chi Minh.

Everything was pleasant and enjoyable, but memories of what had happened during their last excursion kept them from feeling the same exhilaration as before. During this tour they were taken into shops and encouraged to buy souvenirs. Though this seemed hopeful, they reminded each other not to get carried away.

Instead of being interrogated the next day, they were measured for new clothes. All got new shoes, except Betty. They didn't have any women's shoes available in her size, but they took measurements and said they would have a pair custom made for her. Even more exciting, they were told they would be allowed to make tape recordings for broadcast so their families would know they were safe and well. Then they were asked to fill out requests for release.

"What about Paul?" Peter wanted to know.

"Oh, he'll be back soon," Mr. Van replied.

"That's what you said nearly two weeks ago."

"Trust me," was the only reply they could get from their inscrutable overseer. Excited over the prospect of making tapes they pressed no further.

Even LuAnne busied herself writing a letter to her sister and brothers that she could read over the recorder. She could hardly wait to talk to them, but when she stood before the mike, she panicked and couldn't get out a word. After the opportunity had passed she sobbed and sobbed. "Maybe they'll think I'm not with you," she worried. "That I'm somewhere else."

"It's all right, Honey," her mother soothed. "I told them about you and your birthday party and everything, so they'll know we're all together."

Betty tried to get in a message to each of her children. "Gerry, don't worry about me because I am getting plenty of rest. I even have my own pillow and each night before I go to sleep I think of that verse you sent me about sleeping—Psalm 4:8. And, Glenn, I've thought of you so often since I've been here for they have given us some of those green-skinned bananas you like so much. And, Loretta, there are many things that make me think of you because you always loved the out-of-doors. Rocks and flowers and all sorts of things you would love to paint. And I think of you, Becki, at twenty-seven years of age with a year-old daughter. I am reminded that when I was twenty-seven I was in this same place with you when you were one year old. And, David, I want you to take good care of Becki and Rachel for me. I know you will.

"I thank the Lord daily for each of you and I know you have been praying for me, too. I only hope it won't be too long before we are together again."

The written reports and interrogations continued, but they didn't seem quite as difficult until Carolyn came from one to report that she had been told what their crime was.

"You mean they really explained it to you?" John reacted in disbelief.

"Yeah, he really blew his cool. Yelled at me. 'You mean, you really don't know what you have done?' he shouted. 'Why, you have come from your country to teach the Bru people about your religion, and some of them have believed you. You wrote your Bible in their words and taught them to read. And do you think they will forget this just because you are gone from them? Oh, no. They will remember. And even worse, they will tell their children. And their children's children. And some of them will believe. And a hundred years from now, we will still be trying to undo what you have done with these people.' "

"Well, praise the Lord!" John responded. "What a testimony to the power of the gospel of Christ! And coming from a Communist political officer at that."

"I feel it is really significant," Carolyn agreed. "That accusation really put things into perspective for me. I mean, what does it really matter if we should never be released. If we should die, our witness would still live on. No matter what they do to us the years we have invested in Vietnam have been worth it all, for the gospel will continue."

The missionaries were thrilled at this revelation.

"You know," Betty mused, "we have a tendency to say a

field is 'closed' when missionaries are no longer allowed in a country. But the Christians we have left behind will continue to witness. And God's Word has been left in many languages, and it shall continue to do His work. But we must be faithful to pray for our dear brothers and sisters who are left. Their big job is ahead as they spread the news to their own people in spite of the persecution that may come."

This thought encouraged Betty when she was ordered to write a report on the leprosarium. She was working on this one afternoon when she heard an unfamiliar voice yell, "Hey, guys!" She looked up to see Slim running across the courtyard at full speed.

"I can talk!" he announced.

Full of questions, they gathered around the mysterious American: "Who are you?" "Where are you from?" "When were you taken?"

"My name's Jim Lewis. I'm from San Diego, California, I'm with the State Department, and I'm everything the Commies say I am. Man, is it good to talk to you guys! It's been so hard watching you and not being able to join in."

As they welcomed him into the group, they began swapping stories of their experiences in captivity. Jim mentioned his part in evacuating Nhatrang.

"Nhatrang!" both Millers interrupted. "We left three kids in school in Nhatrang. Do you know if they got out?"

"Yes," Jim was able to assure them, "all Americans got out of Nhatrang. I'm positive."

"You don't know how good that is to know," Carolyn said, obviously relieved. "That's the first word we've had in seven months. But they were probably taken to Saigon. Do you know if they got out of there? What about that plane that crashed?"

"There were Americans on that plane. Two friends of mine were killed. As a matter of fact, I saw the manifest and it looked to me that there were more Americans dead than Vietnamese. The orphans were on the upper deck and didn't get it as bad."

"So we really don't know any more than before," John said as the short-lived joy vanished and the old doubts rushed in again.

"Sorry," was all Jim could say.

But Mr. Van had something. "In a few days you could have some good news," he told the group the next day. Despite all their resolutions about not getting their hopes up again, it seemed evident that release was not far off.

The twenty-fourth of October was Loretta Mitchell's twenty-fourth birthday, and Betty celebrated it by filling out two very promising forms. One a request for an exit visa, the other for repatriation to the United States. She was also presented with a new set of clothes and the shoes that had been made for her.

"It really does look as if we might be going home soon," she smiled.

"Well, you missionaries maybe," Jim said. "They might let you go, but they'll keep Paul and me, I'm sure."

The women enthusiastically washed their clothes and got everything ready to leave at a moment's notice. On Sunday they held worship services in the Millers' room. This time Jim was allowed to participate instead of sitting across the courtyard straining to hear what was going on. At Jay's request they sang more than usual, all joining in with gusto. The atmosphere was optimistic as together they sang "Amazing Grace" and "O God, Our Help in Ages Past" and listened to Dick sing "The Love of God."

On Monday, the twenty-seventh, Paul rode into the compound in an old truck. Thrilled over the reunion, they pressured Mr. Van for more definite information about their future.

"In a couple of days you could be released," he admitted.

"Who?" they wanted to know.

"All of you. A ninety-percent chance all of you will be released."

"What about our manuscripts?" Dick asked.

"A ninety-percent chance they will be returned."

Several officials came to the camp for a meeting. "You will be turned over to the United Nations as refugees," they said. "Empty your suitcases and list each item."

They did as instructed and then packed again. Betty was given a new pair of glasses. All of them filled out three more forms for exit visas. Their excitement kept building, yet they had been disappointed so many times they feared becoming overconfident. Then, too, they were concerned that not all the group would be going and that the priceless manuscripts had not been returned.

On Tuesday Betty was again smitten with chills and fever. Her first thought was, "Oh, I can't get sick now. They might hold up our release," and she tried to pretend the symptoms didn't exist.

As the day wore on and she felt worse she confided her condition to Joan.

"Oh, you should get back on the malaria medicine right away," the nurse advised. "I don't think it would make any difference in the plans now. If we are really going to be released the arrangements must have been completed by now. I'll call the medic."

That evening the medic gave Betty some medicine. Before the night was over she was glad she had told. She had more chills and was thankful for the heavy blanket supplied to her. Wednesday her temperature was up but she tried to hide it. Everyone was anxious because Mr. Van said, "Ninety-seven percent chance you will go tomorrow. Everyone."

"They just have to keep us on edge," Norm grumbled. "It wouldn't kill them to let us know what's going on."

Answered Prayers / 227

Later that afternoon they were given sweaters, dark blue or gray, with a bright red one for LuAnne. But there was bad news: the manuscripts would not be returned.

"I am sorry," Mr. Van explained, "but we are not finished examining them yet. When we have completed our study and if we feel there is nothing detrimental to our country in them, we will return them to you."

The Phillipses or the Millers could do nothing about the decision. "Remember what you shared with me when they were taken in Camp Sunshine?" Lil asked.

"I sure do," Carolyn replied. "I've reminded myself of that over and over the past couple of days. We have to just turn them over to the Lord to do with as He sees fit. Perhaps they will really return them to us after we go."

"Do you really think so?" Dick asked.

"Well, I'm not giving up hope," John replied. "The manuscripts are of no value to the North Vietnamese, and they mean so much to us. Maybe they'll give them back."

The prospects of leaving the next morning made it hard to sleep. When awakened at 4:30 A.M. everyone jumped right up, raring to go. The number one question was, How many of them would be leaving? When they were told to board the bus at 6:10 all the foreigners began climbing on.

"I don't understand why they are taking Lewis and me to the airport. I'm sure they aren't going to release us," Paul said.

"Keep still and come on," Norm advised. "Just keep with the group, and maybe you'll make it."

After a two-hour ride to the Hanoi airport the motley group was escorted from the bus and ushered into a VIP room on the upper deck of the terminal. In keeping with oriental custom tea was served while visiting dignitaries and officials chatted with them as if they had been honored guests.

"Well, Mrs. Mitchell," one of the interpreters said, "you

must be very happy to be going home."

"I'm afraid you don't really understand me," Betty replied frankly. "Vietnam has been my home for twenty-seven years and I am really leaving a part of myself here, for I love the Vietnamese people. And the biggest regret is that I never found out anything about my husband. I asked everyone I was able to talk to, but I never found out where he is. I still believe he is alive somewhere."

"If I ever learn anything, I will write you," he promised.

The foreigners had signed each other's tarps that had been issued to them in Camp Sunshine, and now they wrote in a little book for Mr. Van. Betty signed her name and added, "I'll be praying for you."

Mr. Van wrote an inscription in a book of Vietnamese classical literature that had been given to the Millers: "I hope you will never forget these days. The days when we understand each other better than any time before. I wish you and your family happiness and a wonderful reunion."

A meal was served and one of the leading men who had visited them at one of the camps gave a farewell speech. He was "happy" they were able to go back to their families. He "hoped" they would "come back" to visit Vietnam again someday. "In five years everything will be unified and much different from now," he predicted. "You will want to come and see the places where you lived and see how much progress has been made."

Then each of the officials began shaking hands with them. As Mr. Van was saying goodbye to the Johnsons, Norm joked, "Well, it looks as if we are really going. John, you might as well crank up the transmitter we've kept hidden in your sewing machine and radio Washington the escape plans are off. We're coming home via Air Lao."

Jim Lewis turned so pale at Norm's words that Joan thought

he was going to faint. "For God's sake, don't blow it now, Norm! No more kidding," he begged.

Mr. Van just laughed, "Don't worry, Mr. Lewis, Norman just likes to tease. I tell you frankly and sincerely, you are really going home now."

As they came down the stairs a contingent of reporters and photographers waited to record their departure as they were turned over to the United Nations officials and went aboard the Royal Air Lao DC-3, chartered by the UN and bearing the inscription UNITED NATIONS HIGH COMMISSION FOR REFUGEES.

Aloft at last, Paul and Jim could hardly believe they had really been released. The whole group was strangely quiet as they flew west toward Bangkok and freedom. Perhaps their hopes had been dashed too often for them to believe they were actually going, actually returning to their loved ones. It seemed unreal.

As they winged their way westward Betty thought of the many Raday friends she would never see again. Pastor Y-Ngue, Y Ta, the aged Ba Tu, and others. She thought also of Archie, for the plane that was taking her to freedom was taking her further from him.

They landed for refueling in Vientiane, where the refugees were allowed to deplane. As they were being led toward a lounge they caught sight of some old friends. Mennonite missionaries Mary and Luke Martin were standing there beaming. "We had to come to renew our visas," they explained.

"What about our kids?" the Vietnam missionaries asked anxiously.

"They're all safe. They're fine," they reported happily. "The Millers' are in Houghton, New York, with Carolyn's folks, the Phillipses' with Lil's brother in California, the Johnsons' in Canada with Joan's parents.

"And, Betty, Gerry is waiting for you in Bangkok."

"Gerry's in Bangkok!" Betty repeated, hardly daring to believe she had heard correctly.

"Yes, she's been in school in Penang, and they flew her up to be waiting to greet you."

A light seemed to come on in Betty's tired face. She could hardly wait for the trip to continue. Gerry was waiting for her!

Lifted in spirit at the good news, they reboarded for the last leg of the flight. Soon they would be reunited with their children. The dream was coming true.

Excitement increased as the plane neared Bangkok. Besides Gerry, who would be there to greet them?

"Make sure your seat belts are securely fastened, please. Prepare for landing."

Now they were on the runway. Now taxiing toward the terminal and the waiting crowd. The DC-3 had stopped and now they were moving toward the front door.

At the bottom of the stairs each was greeted by his respective ambassador. After that it was all confusion. Carolyn looked for Peter to say goodbye, but he was already in the Australian ambassador's limousine.

The others, still dazed, were directed into an airport bus which quickly made the short trip to the terminal. There a long-haired teenage girl broke loose from the crowd. Cameras clicked and whirred and the waiting crowd cheered as Betty and Gerry melted into each others' arms. The sight of that glad reunion made them realize:

They were free at last!

Dr. Phillips and fellow prisoners are besieged by the press and well-wishers as they step off the airport bus in Bangkok. Behind Phillips are the Johnsons. On the ground, barely visible, Mrs. Phillips is being embraced.
Photo courtesy Alliance Witness

(Bottom left) After months of captivity, Betty Mitchell shares a tearful reunion with daughter Geraldine. (Right) LuAnne Miller holding stuffed dog, a gift from the U.S. Vice Consul upon arrival of prisoners in Bangkok. She brought the doll in the center back from captivity.

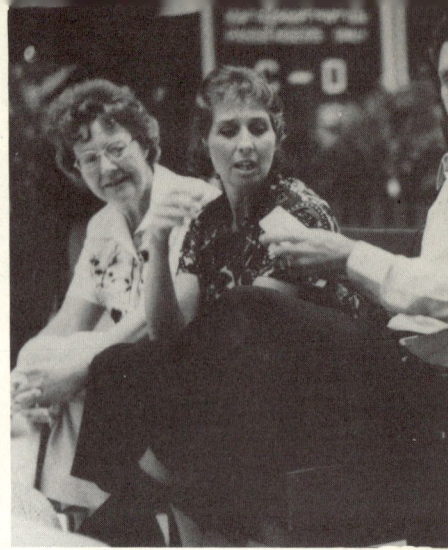

(Left) Betty Mitchell, showing strain from her captivity, talks with daughter Gerry in the VIP room.

Joan and Norman Johnson in departure lounge awaiting flight home. Woman at left is unidentified.

Photo courtesy Alliance Witness

LuAnne, John, and Carolyn Miller shortly after their release from captivity.

Photo courtesy Alliance Witness

Shortly after release, Betty Mitchell looks at pictures while daughter Gerry and Joan and Norman Johnson look on.

Photo courtesy Alliance Witness

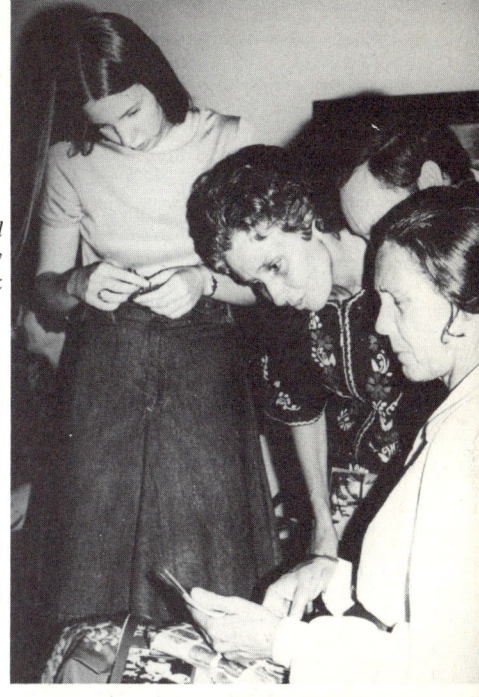

Mr. and Mrs. Johnson and Dr. and Mrs. Phillips in Bangkok after arriving on plane from Hanoi.

Photo courtesy Alliance Witness

Epilogue

For 234 days life had simply stood still for the newly released missionaries, even though those same days were like an eternity. Of primary concern to them had been their children.

The Millers learned that after the fall of Banmethuot, all Wycliffe personnel, including the school children, had been evacuated from Vietnam to the Philippines. Their children remained in the reestablished school until the term ended and then returned to the States at the request of their maternal grandparents, Dr. and Mrs. Stephen Paine.

When the children of the Alliance missionaries at Dalat School in Penang, Malaysia, had learned through a Bangkok newspaper of Banmethuot's fall to the Communists it fell to the dorm parents to keep the children informed. The Woody Stemples and the Ed Manghams carried a deep empathy—Ed had once been a Dalat "kid" himself. Pat and Doug Johnson; Jean, Brian, Ruth, and John Phillips; and Gerry Mitchell had been called to the infirmary and immediately they began to surmise bad news.

"Oh, oh," Ed heard one of the girls say, "we're all from Banmethuot. Something is wrong."

Courageously Ed began, "The Communists are now in control, and we presume your parents are there. We do not know of their whereabouts, but we expect they will get out. When we hear something definite, we'll let you know immediately."

There was no panic. Solemnly and calmly they bore the recognition that they, too, were soldiers and that courage was expected of them as well.

A few days later the children were told that Paul Struharick, a USAID man, had reported by radio that everyone except the Johnsons were safe in his house in Banmethuot. When radio contact was lost, they knew nothing more. It was not until the celebration of Doug Johnson's birthday, April 19, that word was received through the International Control Commission that the missionaries had been seen alive.

As time wore on and the Vietnam situation worsened, nothing else seemed important to the Banmethuot MKs but the safety of their parents. And the other children at Dalat School centered their concern with them, especially after all missionaries had been accounted for except the ones from Banmethuot.

Even though Gerry had not heard from her father for thirteen years and now her mother had similarly been taken captive, she revealed an inner peace.

"Don't worry, they'll be back. The Lord is taking care of Mom," she often reassured the others.

Those at the school found comfort in sharing the promise of Second Chronicles 30:9: *"For if you turn again unto the Lord, your brothers and your children [parents, too] shall find compassion before them that led them captive, and shall come again into this land."* Someone noted the conditional *if* and also that the time of release was not given, but they agreed that the release could take some time

On October 5, at the close of Spiritual Emphasis Week, a gracious revival moved in upon the Dalat students and faculty. Confessions and requests for forgiveness resulted in a renewed faith in the promise of Second Chronicles because the conditional *if* carried new and real meaning. A few days later one of the teachers, Pauline Inghram, was reading Isaiah 51:14 from the American Standard Version of the Bible when a phrase seemed to spring to her attention: *"The captives will soon be released."*

The various prayer groups claimed the promise. Within two weeks the United Nations announced that the captives would be freed.

Betty's children in California had experienced sudden shock at the news of her capture. As Becki was watching NBC's Today show the newscaster announced that Banmethuot had been overrun and that the missionaries were stranded. Immediately she had called her husband, David, and Loretta and Glenn. They gathered for prayer, and later friends from the church they attended joined with them. Together they trusted God for miracles in that far-off city that had seen so much tragedy.

Becki's little daughter Rachel did not yet understand that her paternal grandparents, the Ed Thompsons, were buried in that city or that her maternal grandfather had been taken captive many years ago or that her grandmother was now in grave danger. But the sacrifice represented in this grandchild's relationships touched thousands of Christians, compelling them to intercede unceasingly for God's intervention.

That all the captives survived the ordeal can be attributed only to prevailing prayer. When the sound of familiar voices met over the telephone, their joy of anticipated reunion could not dim their consciousness of God's goodness and faithfulness.

When asked to express their feelings, Carolyn replied, "Scripture says it best: *'When the Lord turned again the captivity of Zion, we were like them that dream. Then was our mouth filled with laughter, and our tongue with singing: then said they among the heathen, The Lord hath done great things for them: The Lord hath done great things for us; whereof we are glad'"* (Ps. 126:1-3).

Betty added, "I love the Lord Jesus more than ever."

The American missionaries spent their first night of freedom at the Alliance Guest Home and the Canadians became special guests of their government officials. They were somewhat apprehensive as to how they would adjust to comfortable beds after sleeping on bamboo for so long, but, as it turned out, they managed beautifully.

The next day each excitedly reported to the others the experiences of the night before.

"I had a bubble bath! Can you believe it? A nice, hot, relaxing bubble bath," reported Joan.

The Johnsons described how the whole Canadian Embassy staff had accompanied them to a fancy restaurant where they were told to order anything they wished to eat. After they had looked at the elaborate menu they had ordered hamburgers.

"Man, were they good!" exclaimed Norm.

Amid the excitement of fellowship among friends they had not seen for so long and arranging for visas, passports, and picture taking, there arose a shadow of solemnity when Betty's physical condition worsened. Keyed by the impending release and the exciting events, Betty had ignored malaria symptoms and the delicate balance toward recovery was suddenly reversed. She was quickly shuttled to the Adventist hospital by ambulance.

The anticlimactic encounter deeply affected Gerry who attended her mother, but three days later, on November 5—Glenn's twenty-second birthday—Betty improved and was brought back to the Guest Home. After a time she was strong enough to go to Malaysia to finish recuperating while Gerry completed her term in school before Christmas vacation.

The Phillipses had a joyful reunion with their children in

California and then flew to Minneapolis where a grand welcome had been planned by friends. The newspapers gave them front-page billing, and television and radio reporters competed for interviews. But first attention was given to a special couple, former missionaries to India now in their eighties, Lil's parents.

As the Johnsons' plane approached the Toronto airport, a familiar melody came from the sound system. "Listen, Joan!" Norm almost shouted. "They're playing our song, 'Release Me.' "

In the crowd that welcomed them were their children, parents, and other relatives. The mayor of their hometown, Hamilton, Ontario, had arranged an impressive reception at the city hall.

"Boy," chortled Norm to Joan, "this is some homecoming for a guy who used to collect garbage in this town."

The Millers arrived at the Buffalo, New York, airport for a grand reunion. From there they were escorted to Houghton where the streets were lined with torch-bearing students of Houghton College, their alma mater. LuAnne was soon enrolled in school where she received kind attention by the principal and teachers. Her rapid adjustment assured everyone that she seemed to bear no scars, emotionally or otherwise, from the months in captivity.

Betty's reunion with Becki, David, and Rachel came just a few days before Christmas when she and Gerry flew to France. The Thompsons were there for language study. After the first flush of greeting Becki spoke in measured words, "I heard the news, but I couldn't believe you had been released until I saw you on the TV screen coming off the plane. I looked, and there was my bony mom. Then I looked over your shoulder to see Dad, but he wasn't there. All the time we had felt he would be coming back with you."

After the tears had dried, Becki and David shared their plans that since Cambodia had fallen to the Communists, they were assigned to serve as medical missionaries in Gabon.

From France Betty and Gerry flew to Nyack, New York, where Betty met with the headquarters staff who had fervently prayed and worked in behalf of the missionaries held captive. Then they flew on to California for a short visit with Loretta and Glenn and up the coast to Oregon for a reunion with Betty's and Archie's families.

Extensive medical checkups revealed that all the missionaries were in remarkably good health. All of them had lost weight during their captivity, Betty having lost the most—fifty-five pounds. The doctors predicted that damage to Norm's optic nerves due to protein deficiency would correct itself.

The released missionaries have been in touch with several of their fellow captives. Jay is in Cornell University graduate school, Peter is back in Australia, and Paul lives with his family in Washington, D. C., where he is assigned to the United States Agency for International Development. Jim Lewis and the two Filipinos, Ike and Bog, have not been heard from yet, but the missionaries continue to pray for each one of them as well as for the Communist officers and guards and Vietnamese POWs in the various prison camps.

Flooded with requests for interviews and speaking engagements, they often relive the memories of their experiences. Norm, who had vowed during his captivity to forget it all, found he could not keep his vow. "I just have to praise God for all He has done for us!" he says.

Convinced that prayer had brought them safely home, their gratitude goes to concerned Christians of all denominations and churches who upheld them in prayer. Frequently, when asked to summarize their experience, they quote Second Corinthians 1:8-11 from the *Living Bible:*

I think you ought to know, dear brothers, about the hard time we went through in Asia. We were really crushed and overwhelmed, and feared we would never live through it. We felt we were doomed to die and saw how powerless we were to help ourselves; but that was good, for then we put everything into the hands of God, who alone could save us, for he can even raise the dead. And he did help us, and saved us from a terrible death; yes, and we expect him to do it again and again. But you must help us too, by praying for us. For much thanks and praise will go to God from you who see his wonderful answers to your prayers for our safety!

In spite of the hardships endured, the released missionaries are grateful for the humanitarian treatment they received from their captors. They provided food and medicine though often it was hard to obtain, and they did not subject them to needless physical abuse. They still hope for the return of the priceless manuscripts which represented years of labor by the Phillipses and Millers.

Would the "prisoners of hope" be willing to return to Vietnam if the new government would permit it? Each emphatically answers, "YES!"

John Miller embraces sons Gordon (l.) and Nathan at Greater Buffalo International Airport eighteen days after being released from captivity in Vietnam.

Photo courtesy Wide World Photos

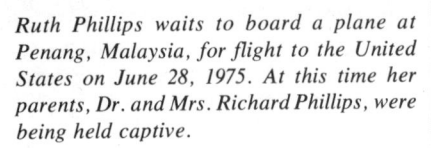

Ruth Phillips waits to board a plane at Penang, Malaysia, for flight to the United States on June 28, 1975. At this time her parents, Dr. and Mrs. Richard Phillips, were being held captive.

The Phillips children in home of relatives in Yucaipa, Calif., while their parents were held captive in Vietnam.

Photo courtesy Redlands Daily Facts

Carolyn and John Miller were welcomed home in Houghton, N.Y., by torchlight parade. Shown here are the Millers' children. LuAnne, who was taken captive with them, is on Mr. Miller's left.

Ordeal over but not forgotten, Lillian and Richard Phillips with their children at the Yucaipa (Calif.) home of Lillian's brother. Memorabilia of life in prison camps include hats, lantern, rice bowl and spoon, teapot, and cups.
Photo courtesy L.A. Times

The Norman Johnson family reunited in Ontario after parents' release from captivity.
Photo courtesy Toronto Star

Joan Johnson enjoying moment with children, Doug and Pat.
Photo by Roy Farrell

Norman Johnson sharing tearful moment with daughter, Pat, and mother, Mrs. E. Johnson, during reunion in Ontario.
Photo by Roy Farrell

Mrs. E. Johnson with son Norman soon after his release from captivity.
Photo by Roy Farrell

Lillian Phillips is greeted on arrival at Minneapolis-St. Paul airport by her parents, Rev. and Mrs. Tilman Amstutz.
Photo courtesy Minneapolis Tribune

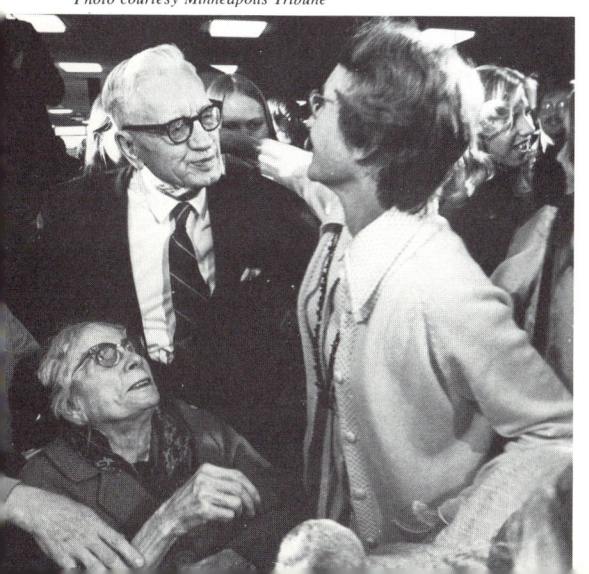

Richard and Lillian Phillips being interviewed by news media personnel at the Minneapolis-St. Paul airport in November 1975 after being reunited with relatives and friends.

Dr. and Mrs. Phillips after reunion with children in California. Phillips shows board for playing Scrabble, one of the games he made to occupy time during imprisonment.
Photo courtesy Redlands Daily Facts